LET THE CHILDREN PAINT: Art in Religious Education

KATHRYN S. WRIGHT

The Seabury Press • New York

Acknowledgments

Grateful acknowledgment is made to the following publishers for permission to use copyrighted material from the titles listed:

Doubleday & Company, Inc.—G. Ernest Wright and Reginald H. Fuller, *The Book of the Acts of God*. Copyright © 1957 by G. Ernest Wright

Harcourt, Brace & World, Inc.—C. S. Lewis, *Surprised by Joy*.

The Macmillan Company—Viktor Lowenfeld, *Your Child and His Art*. Copyright © 1954.

Charles Scribner's Sons—Fleming James, *Personalities of the Old Testament*.

The Living Church Foundation, Inc.—*The Living Church*, June 13, 1965.

David McKay Company, Inc.—John Oxenham, *The Hidden Years*.

World Council of Christian Education—Paul Tillich, "Creative Love in Education," *World Christian Education*, Second Quarter, 1949.

All children's names in this book are fictitious.

**To all the children and teachers
who helped to make this book**

PREFATORY NOTE

My indebtedness is great to colleagues and friends, both past and present, but especially to:

Elizabeth Feist, whose teaching revealed to me how art can help to bring good news to children at the deeper levels of their lives;

The children who contributed the illustrations;

The Riverside Church, for the opportunity to include a weekday painting session in the church school program;

Mary Elizabeth Thompson, for her generous sharing of experience with children's art in Oregon;

Margaret and James Adams, Peggy Cooley, Barbara Noland, Barnett Shepherd, and Barbara Withers, for sharing results of their experiments in creative expression;

Lillian Williams, for her suggestions on art reproductions;

The Children's Work Committee of the Synod of Oregon, the United Presbyterian Church in the U.S.A., for permission to use the painting "God and My Grandpa";

The Manhattan Division of the Protestant Council, for the opportunity to work with teachers and children of the inner city.

CONTENTS

Prefatory Note   4

Part I:
Painting in Religious Education
1 For Joy   9
2 For Acceptance   18
3 For Growth and Understanding   28
4 For Fellowship   42
5 For Appreciation   58
6 In Any Kind of Parish   70

Part II:
Practical Helps for the Teacher
7 Procedures   89
   When to Paint   89
   Who Should Paint?   90
   Where to Paint   90
   Setting Up the Room   91
   Materials   92
   The First Session   93
   The Second Session   96

	Summary of Proposed Sessions	98
	Check List of Supplies	100
8	Guidance	101
	Is Training Necessary?	101
	Introductory Workshop for Teachers	103
	Indirect and Direct Guidance	107
	Tryout-Period Experiments	109
	Warning!	111
	Some Useful Pointers	111
9	Subject Matter	113
	The Relationship of Themes	125
10	Using Resources Effectively	128
	Books	131
	Films	144
	Recordings	147
	Slides	148
	Television	149
	Traveling Exhibits	149

Appendix:
Biblical Stories Related to Themes and Hymns	150
Painting Projects	154
Pictures	158
Museums in the United States	161
Where to Order Reproductions	162
Author's Notes	164
General Bibliography	166

Illustrations Follow Page 80

PART I

Painting
in Religious Education

CHAPTER 1

FOR JOY

"The chief end of man," runs an ancient catechism, "is to glorify God and enjoy him forever." One way to give children the opportunity to do both is to let them paint—not merely to rub crayon between the lines of a prescribed "lesson" picture on an activity sheet, but freely to paint with color and a brush.

To discover or develop a medium of creative expression is exciting at any age, but there is a special reason for offering it to children of the first six grades: they are still, especially in the first four grades, and somewhat in the fifth and sixth, in touch with their unstudied thought and true feeling, and unless emotionally blocked, they are more likely to make a spontaneous response to an idea than a "correct" one. They are more likely to be original and less likely to imitate. Moreover, if given the opportunity to be creative before adolescence, they may retain something of this open, childlike quality to enrich their teen-age days when logic and the critical faculties must develop more fully. In fact, through the practice of visual arts, the "intense and delighted vision of a young child" can not only be preserved but "recreated if it has been destroyed in earlier years." [1] Whether this happens or not, however, if children have any "rights," one of them is the right to joy. If a person has not known joy as a child, he will be deprived all his life no matter how many other advantages may be heaped upon him.

True joy is in direct contact with God, and requires no words to affirm it, for it is in itself a state of grace. Words of praise and thanksgiving may follow, but they are not required as evidence, being rather the overflow from a cup that is already full. One little girl who had just turned six, and was attending vacation church school for the first time, seemed to be enjoying this kind of grace one morning as she sat back and surveyed the work of her hands, a lovely combination of colors in a charming arrangement of her own imagining. The teacher saw that a moment of truth had arrived for Betty and moved over quietly to ask if she would like to say anything about her work.

"Yes," said Betty without embarrassment, "I just want to say, 'Oh, it's fun, God.' "

If a painting expresses this kind of joy, it will be religious in value, whether it contains a visible religious symbol or not, because it has been deeply felt in relation to value beyond oneself, and requires original creative activity. Line drawings of religious symbols may be valid to help children recognize and understand the symbols, but to copy such drawings by hand or fill them in with crayon does not constitute a true experience either of art or of religion. Actually, they might be called signs rather than symbols, because they point to a meaning but do not contain an expression of meaning within themselves. They are diagrams to remind us, they do not portray. On the other hand, Van Gogh's "Starry Night" expresses a religious attitude toward reality but contains no "sign" specifically pointing to something else. The whole picture has itself a spiritual meaning.

In a large city church on the Sunday after Easter, a young teacher sat in a circle playing a game with early comers in a fourth-grade class. When the group was as complete as it was likely to be, he led the children to talk about plans for the morning. Joanna raised her hand.

"Can we paint today?" she asked shyly.

"What would you like to paint?" the teacher responded.

"The joy of Easter," she said, her eyes shining.

The other children agreed enthusiastically, and without further motivation materials were set up with the children's help, and the painting began. A hum of contentment filled the room, reminding one of the motto "I sing behind the plow," [2] because there was such a clear sense of being in touch with the source of abundant life. When it was time to stop for worship that morning, the tables and floor had blossomed into as many interpretations of the Resurrection as there were children in the class. Joanna, who had previously confined herself to pale and timid strokes, had burst into a full page of golden yellow decorated by a graceful border of gayly colored flowers. She did not have to draw an angel with a lily to prove that she knew something of Easter.

True, the story intended for this day had to be omitted, but the teacher had made a quick choice in the light of Joanna's unexpected question, and the results assured him it had been a wise one. The worship that day seemed like an extension of the painting session, for both, after all, had been a time of adoration and thanksgiving for the joy of Easter.

Children need joy. It is their element. In it they can live and move and have their being, as Jesus must have known when he gave them his special invitation to a blessing: "for to such belongs the kingdom of God." Grownups are invited to this celebration too, for the records of our faith are full of admonitions to shout and sing for joy; they abound in stories of great events, from the Exodus to Easter, which brought rejoicing to the world. If deliverance can bring joy, perhaps joy can help to bring deliverance. Yet we often seem surprised by it, as if it were an unearned increment, which of course it is, and one we seldom really count on; or as if we expect to be called on to glorify God occasionally but not to enjoy him often, certainly not "forever"! We do not fully comprehend or believe in grace. Perhaps this is why we have failed to provide adequately for enjoyment in our work with children.

During the next decade, possibly far beyond, our revolutionary era will exact a heavy toll of uncertainty and confusion from everyone alive, including our children. As our world is shaken and our old values are challenged, parents and educators will be searching ever more desperately for those elements in life which are excellent beyond question and hence worthy of our permanent allegiance. Joy is one of these essentials. Without it, as without love, life for children becomes meaningless. With it, children will be better prepared to solve the problems life presents, for it is as important to the spirit as food is to the body.

How shall we provide this essential ingredient? There are many kinds of creative expression that will help, of course, but as we have already indicated, painting is one of the most meaningful. Teachers and committees skeptical of taking painting seriously in Christian education might find it helpful to visit a day nursery or kindergarten when children are so engaged. They cannot fail to be impressed by the children's interest and absorption in the activity, an involvement which is often so complete that the presence of a visitor is scarcely noticed. The short film called *The Purple Turtle*[3] conveys a vivid impression of the intense interest which painting can stimulate. This film is well worth viewing.

The preschool visit should be followed if possible by one in a vacation church school where primary and junior teachers have already learned what working with color and brush can do for children of six to twelve. If such an opportunity is not available, perhaps a visit to a public or private day school could be arranged. There may be intense concentration in the room, or purposeful movement back and forth to sink or cupboard, or quiet conversation between the teacher and a pupil asking for help; or there could be, depending on the size and location of the school, a tremendous buzz of chatter, with bursts of enthusiasm and surprise. Exceptions are always possible, but unless there are special conditions not yet solved (such as too many children for the size of the room, not enough assistance, or inadequate equipment), one is not likely to find serious problems of discipline. The children are usually too happy for that. They are in touch with reality, creating something which is their own, which they have chosen, something which involves their mind, their imagination, and even a certain amount of relaxed and assured bodily movement. They are engaged in a highly individual activity, but it is one that does not isolate them from the group. Something worthwhile is going on for everyone in the room and this without regard to the degree of talent he may possess. Everyone in the room can hold a brush and everyone can put color on paper in some fashion, and in ways that will be different from anything ever put down on paper before. Each is learning in some measure to know himself, and to achieve identity and a growing sense of significance.

Moreover, to a child (as to an adult), it is fascinating to watch one's work grow under the hand, bringing surprises and discoveries of many kinds. Shapes and lines and swirls take form quite unpredictably at first, and occasionally there is a design or shape of unmistakable beauty, leading even the timid to venture farther out, like a novice cutting his first figures on the ice.

Color is another enchanting discovery. There is that brilliant glowing dish of red to be transferred to paper—as much of it as you wish, and at your own speed. Then, whenever you want, you may wash your brush and dip it into the blue or the yellow. Or you can leave the pure color for a bit and experiment with mixing colors of your own. You are in charge of what happens on this particular sheet of paper. Discoveries in shape and line and color go on and on, until all too soon it is time to lay the paintings aside to dry. Now comes the moment to sum up what you have done in your own words as the teacher takes them down. You feel you have accomplished something, like putting words to music or saying "Amen" to a prayer. When the paintings are dry, they will be put up on the bulletin board or hung on a wire with clothespins. YOURS may be there the next time you come. Shout for joy and praise the Lord!

Although children have a capacity for joy, they need help

to experience it, help from someone who is himself enriched by joy and concerned that it be made available as far as possible to every child under his care. Without the stimulus of a parent or some other concerned adult, the door to the joy of painting may remain closed, perhaps forever. Skill alone is not enough to open this door, nor is it merely a matter of placing supplies where children can reach them. Someone has to love a child to bring him joy—love him creatively, not sentimentally. The most complete revelation of this kind of love is found in the New Testament, where it is called *agape* to distinguish it from less Godlike expressions of interest and concern. Agape is a quality of love that has the power to accept a person just as he is and to start him on the way to a new and fulfilling life.

Does this sound a little lofty for children? We can be sure it would not to Jesus. He would not have used those words, nor should we, perhaps (and certainly not with children), but children can experience their meaning through his spirit and his action. Nolde, the modern German artist, has painted a picture of this kind of love in his "Jesus Among the Children." [4] Turning his back upon the critical disciples, whose figures are done in black, Jesus stoops to pick up a toddler who is throwing his arm around Jesus' neck. Other children and infants with their mothers crowd around and press forward, their lively, eager eyes seeking out his face. There is an earthy quality in the faces and figures, which are done with strong tones of red and yellow predominating, and the children, who by some standards might be called untidy, remind us that Jesus was concerned with people rather than appearances, which may be one reason why the people heard him gladly. One little fellow, scantily clad, is reaching up confidently to grasp Jesus by the arm, wanting his attention, wanting to touch him, expecting to be loved.

What a painting to hang in the board room of a church, especially when officials are approaching a decision on budget priorities, or in a director's office when the hours become inhuman, or in a teacher's home as the stewardship of her abilities begins to be more costly.

But there is more to say of joy. There is the room without windows in the basement of a church in a crowded slum. It is lighted only by a bare electric bulb, but here a dozen boys and girls gather after a long day in school, eager for the chance to paint. There is the child in a residential area who asks to come early to help prepare the room for painting. There is the second-grade girl in a mid-western church who uses magenta for the first time. She stumbles on it in an experiment while painting a scene for a puppet show on Nehemiah, and she keeps repeating the word over and over rhythmically as she dips her brush and paints: "Mah-jen-tah, mah-jen-tah. I shall use mah-jen-tah." It sounds like a poem. Or those children in Harlem and on the Lower East Side of New York who are not satisfied to paint for one hour; they want to stay for two. Or the boy in the suburb, "devilish and uninhibited," his teacher called him with affection, who portrayed with great gusto and charm his idea of the stormy wind mentioned in Psalm 148. Or the girl in the country who drew an exaggerated donkey for the entry into Jerusalem, explaining, "I like to draw horses. When I think of the Bible, that's the thing I think of most!" Or the boy in a Pentecostal church who became so excited when he accidentally mixed two colors that he called to everyone to share his discovery. "Look what's happening," he shouted. "The colors are changing. Come quick!" And sure enough, the blue was vanishing and so was the red, and the purple was being born. And, finally, the small child in a far-western city who painted children close to Jesus, explaining, "The children are jumping for joy."

The most abundant source for paintings of joy and wonder by children, however, is the Christmas material, which encompasses one perfect drama of human need and divine fulfillment, yet is made up of many smaller ones, like precious jewels in a royal crown.

Each year during the Advent Season we have the unspeakable privilege of conducting our children through this "holy history"—from the ancient longing of the Hebrews for deliverance to the good news of great joy for all people. We read the great, majestic words of Scripture together and are moved by their meaning to sing, to dramatize, and to worship. Let us also paint.

There are many moments of the Event from which to choose, and we need not paint them all. How many and which ones will depend on the interests of the children and their leader. Yet as we recall the matchless story we wonder how we can leave out any of them.

"The people who walked in darkness have seen a great light. . . . In the sixth month the angel Gabriel was sent from God. . . . My soul doth magnify the Lord, and my spirit hath rejoiced in God my Saviour. . . . And Joseph also went up from Galilee . . . unto the city of David . . . and she gave birth to her first-born son and wrapped him in swaddling cloths, and laid him in a manger . . . and in that region there were shepherds out in the field. . . . And lo, the star which they had seen in the East went before them, till it came to rest over the place where the child was . . . and they fell down and worshiped him."

In one church, where the children had become deeply interested, they actually did paint all the events referred to above. The work was done over a period of time, some on Sunday morning, more during a weekday class after school. One older junior was inspired by Isaiah and the words of an Advent hymn to paint an abstract called "O come, O come, Emmanuel, and ransom captive Israel." There was a black portion for the darkness and evil in the world, green for hope, and a red flame symbolizing the power of love to come. When a younger junior completed her interpretation of the Annunciation story, she had been so moved by the experience that she could only say, "I have no words for it."

A still younger girl, who wanted to show Mary's happiness when she heard the angel's message, said simply: "Mary is happy. This is her feeling." A boy of ten depicted a tremendous radiance pouring from a manger, with a tiny figure kneeling at each end. "This is the holy light that came with his birth," he said. "Mary and Joseph were there." A girl of the same age presented the journey of the three wise men under a night sky of depth and mystery. Her comment reflected the wonder of it: "They are all tired, but they never stop. The nearer they come to the stable, the lighter it gets."

The journey to Bethlehem, whether by the wise men or Mary and Joseph, is a well-loved theme at Christmas. The idea of Mary riding the donkey, Joseph leading the way, and both pushing on in spite of weariness, not knowing there will be no room for them at the inn, appeals strongly to children's respect for human courage and tenderness, as well as to their sense of suspense. An unusual portrayal was made by one eleven-year-old girl who went beyond the human qualities in the drama to a cosmic emphasis. She showed the figures approaching the town, but overhead were white rays of light fanning out from the sky. Her verbal explanation was: "The white is the joy of all nature for the event which is going to happen."

Apparently a young schoolgirl had caught something of the same spirit as the Hebrew poet when he rejoiced with all creation at the fulfillment of God's purpose:

> Sing, O heavens, for the LORD has done it;
>   shout, O depths of the earth;
> break forth into singing, O mountains,
>   O forest, and every tree in it!
> For the LORD has redeemed Jacob,
>   and will be glorified in Israel.
>
> *Isaiah 44:23*

CHAPTER 2

FOR ACCEPTANCE

All children need to know they are accepted, first in their own home, then by new adult friends as their world expands. Even though a child may always have had the security of being welcomed, so that he need never know the lonely burden of the "unwanted," he still has to contend with the lesser rejections, real or imagined, which trouble every human being from time to time.

No parents are perfect, and even with the best intentions may fail through ignorance or misplaced ambition to accept their children as they are rather than as they wish they were. It is not uncommon for a well-fed, supposedly happy child to know the fear of failure or inadequacy. He may fear not being liked by other children or not pleasing his teacher, or he may fear he will fail to satisfy his parents' hopes for him in grades or games or even good looks.

The Sunday church school often has the privilege of being the first influence beyond the home, and it is important that the arrangements be planned with intelligent concern. The quality of these early contacts at the church will affect the lifelong attitude of a child toward people, the Church, and the God in whom its members profess to believe. It is no accident that on

Sunday mornings nursery and kindergarten rooms increasingly offer children an opportunity to paint, for this is an accepting kind of activity. It involves the sort of "messing about" that children enjoy but used to be denied because it was "too much trouble" or took "too much time." Unfortunately this attitude still prevails in a majority of church schools above the preschool level.

It is hardly necessary to say that there are many other ways of letting a child know he "belongs" at church, but because painting is one of the best and because it has been so ignored in both planning and training, a strong statement in its behalf is due in the interest of the children and their Christian nurture. As a creative act, painting involves a great deal of a child: his feelings, his memory of past experiences, his thoughts and ideas, his observation of the world around him, even a degree of bodily movement as he lets his arm swing the brush across the paper. When he is allowed to paint freely, his work is a part of *him* and must be respected as such. A wise teacher will appreciate the work of each child for its own sake instead of making comparisons with that of other children, and she will evaluate each child's painting by what it means to the child rather than by an arbitrary standard of artistic excellence. She will not say, "That's a good painting, Jim." She will ask him to tell her about the picture himself. Children's paintings are neither "good" nor "bad" by adult standards in a judgmental sense. They are what they are, a child's personal expression, and they do not need to be justified. They need to be accepted and, if possible, understood. There should be no pushing for an end product in adult terms. Such an objective would be unnatural for primary and junior children, who have ways of thought and expression that are their own and that are right for them. For this age-group the primary value of painting lies in what happens to each child in the doing. Since the picture itself is important as a record of that doing, however, and a visible sign of the doer's achievement and value as a person, it is more helpful to think of the act of painting and the product not as two separate elements, but as two parts of a related whole. What happened in a children's center will clarify the point. A young boy from Haiti, who knew little English, could speak the language of painting as well as anyone in the group. When his paintings were proudly shared with others at a closing program, their meaning was extended by the giving and receiving of the recognition which took place. Yet the motive for painting was not the exhibit; it was to provide the fullest opportunity for growth all along the way.

During a vacation school in a crowded city parish, primary children took a trip to the park after discussing the story of creation. When they returned, they had a painting session. Several made pictures of flowers "because God created them"; others painted their church "because God has something to do with it." The young teacher was gratified by the colorful results, but she was puzzled by Tommy's picture, which was filled with odd shapes resembling animals and trees and other things not too readily identifiable, but all dominated by the large, smiling face of a boy obviously rather like himself.

"But Tommy," said the teacher, without really thinking, "the others painted pretty flowers and churches."

Tommy stood his ground. "God created us too, didn't he?"

The young teacher, brought up short, was learning fast that day. "You're right, Tommy," she said. "You're absolutely right."

That afternoon, in an evaluation period with a colleague, she realized how unfair it would have been to reprove Tommy for being different from the others. He had shown originality and had the courage to defend it, and what he was apparently trying to portray was all six days of creation instead of only one. The teacher saw that these were abilities to be encouraged, that to deny them would be to deny Tommy's creativity, a portion of the image of God.

A tryout period before the major painting of the day is a splendid opportunity for children to get acquainted with their materials. This should often be a free time, with no set tasks or motivation other than a casual "see how your brush feels on your paper. Try all kinds of lines or shapes. Try any color you want. Mix a new color. Have fun!"

This accepting attitude creates a glorious sense of freedom in the room as children go ahead with their experiments and discoveries. Without realizing it, they will be letting thoughts and feelings well up out of their past experiences to be transferred in form and color to the paper. Or, if they are more experienced, they may consciously experiment with mixing tints and shades or try their hand at abstract designs. Beginners like to drop paint of different colors on wet paper or try it on dry paper and fold it over to see what happens. Effects are unpredictable and sometimes beautiful. In any case, when they learn that an accidental splash will not evoke the teacher's wrath, or that an old shirt of Father's will keep their clothes acceptable to Mother, they can relax and take their fun in stride.

Free painting is in itself a kind of therapy, but it can also reveal a need for help that might not otherwise be discovered. Such was the case with Maria, aged eight, whose paintings had puzzled her teacher because of the continued presence in them of sharp, jagged lines in heavy red and black, in contrast to the more cheerful colors chosen by the other children. Finally a call in the home revealed that Maria's mother had an obvious preference for an older daughter, reason enough to cause feelings of rejection and hostility. Because of the mother's domineering manner, the teacher felt it unlikely that Maria would express resentment openly at home, even if she could admit such a feeling to herself. Teachers are haunted by countless problems such as this, which children themselves can neither express nor understand. They blindly ask for help, like the lines from Tennyson's "In Memoriam":

> Who am I?
> An infant crying in the night;
> An infant crying for the light;
> With no language but a cry.

Painting can be an outlet for releasing feelings that cannot be safely or acceptably released elsewhere. By the end of the term, Maria was occasionally choosing brighter colors and more curving lines in her art expression. A call in the home followed by other personal contacts, including a visit by the mother to the class, where she saw how well Maria was regarded by her teacher and her classmates, apparently had helped to open the mother's eyes to her daughter as a person.

More difficult to give acceptance to is the child whose well-meaning but overly strict parents sincerely believe that the best way to punish a misdemeanor and assure satisfactory behavior on Sunday morning is to give the child a "good beating" before he leaves the house. If they are not willing to take another look at such a policy, they are not likely to consider professional guidance either, and the teacher must keep searching for imaginative ways to break through both to the child and to his parents, so sorely in need of knowing that the Church does not require perfection of anyone for admission. In such a situation, any creative activity will help a child relax enough to get at least a taste of what it is like to be himself. It is painting, however, that offers more than most activities in healing quality and in variety. The possibilities in color and subject and style are endless, whether the need for expression is an emergency or the common one for every child's happiness and health.

Those who have included painting in their work with children will recall their own discoveries of how significant it can be in unusual circumstances. A colleague in another city tells this heart-warming story: William, who had been blind for several years, indicated his desire to paint with other junior children at his church. He was made welcome, possibly after some misgiving as to the effect his presence might have on his classmates as well as on himself. But the leader's cordial reception created a warm climate of friendliness and trust. The boy could remember the look of color from his sighted days, and the teacher gave him a brush and a set of three colors, guiding his hands at the beginning to show him their position.

William listened carefully to the suggestion that each choose something about his own church to paint, something he especially liked or remembered, something he had heard or done there, or perhaps a thought or feeling about it. William began to fill the top of his large sheet of paper with a confident blue sky, and as he painted, a look of such rapture lighted his face that the leader could scarcely bear the glory of it. William belonged in spite of his handicap, and was taking the first step in a thrilling new adventure. Someday he might enjoy hearing about a painting in the E. B. Crocker Art Gallery, in Sacramento, California, called "Christ Healing the Blind." It is by the School of Van Dyck. In this painting the compassion of Christ is received by the blind man in trust and joy. William might come to understand, through his own experience, that healing need not always be physical.

An all-Negro class at a church center was working on a unit to establish self-identity in relation to the fatherhood of God. It was called "Who Am I?" and one day the children made portraits of themselves on manila paper. They had great fun telling each other whether the paintings were good likenesses or not. They giggled at Susan's because she had put one eye up in her forehead, and laughed at Jimmy's because his ears were at the top of his head. Mary had portrayed herself with long lashes on her demurely closed eyes, "like she's an angel or something." The most interesting thing of all, however, none of the children noticed. While several had outlined their faces with the brown color resembling their own lovely skin tone, others had used red or blue or green, and one had scrubbed white crayon heavily over the entire face. How much more difficult self-acceptance is for some children than for others! This little "white-faced" boy was in double jeopardy, for not only did he have rejection to contend with on a racial basis, but also at home, where his younger brother was a handicapped child and required the lion's share of his mother's attention. No wonder he was known as a troublemaker in the class. His problem was staggering, and although painting could reveal his need, it would not be enough to solve it completely. On the whole, however, this group was a well-adjusted one and entered happily into the art experience. To save the most encouraging part of the story for last, one boy of eight, who had arrived at a place of enviable security within himself, had covered his face completely with brown and in a charming way that resembled the character of a modern African sculpture. He was, moreover, an adopted child, and his sense of security spoke favorably of his adoptive parents.

In helping children to discover and accept themselves, painting can be combined with creative writing to advantage.[1] For example, a primary group might begin a unit on the Creation with a conversation as to how the world began. If children are free to express their own thoughts rather than to repeat set answers they have been told, the exchange of ideas can be lively and absorbing. If the teacher takes down the ideas on a large sheet of paper as the children express them, she can then hang the paper on the bulletin board and read it back, to the children's great delight. The following account of creation was the combined work of a first and second grade during a vacation school: "God put the universe together. He made the dirt first. He put together the sun. He put together Venus and Mercury and all the planets. He fixed the sun so it could give light. He put together the stars. The waters. He put Earth together. He put together even the trees. Then he could put together the animals, because they need the grass and leaves. . . . He put together gravity and made people. God made Adam and Eve. He made men so that men too could make things. God made Henry. He made me and you. And everyone."

Henry was the ever-present child-with-a-problem in this group and was singled out by his classmates for special mention without apology or embarrassment. Perhaps it was in recognition of the mysterious ways of God that the group accepted him more fully than ever before. If God could make Henry, they could accept him.

During worship at the end of that day, the Biblical version of the creation story was read aloud from the first chapter of Genesis, and the children listened with keen interest and attention. They seemed to feel they had a stake in the story now. When they had a painting session the next day, the "six days" of Genesis were reviewed, and free choice was given as to the day each child would portray. Some chose the moon and stars; some, fish or birds or growing things. One boy painted a full-sized portrait with the title: "Me Myself." It would make a good story to say this was Henry discovering his identity for his own good and that of others, but it was not. It was, however, a wholesome affirmation for the boy who did paint it. When self-discovery is seen in relation to God as Creator, a child can begin to see that regardless of his color, or other ways in which he may be different from the majority in his group, the answer to the question "Who Am I?" is nothing less than "a child of God."

One day at a children's center in an urban mission church where painting is popular on weekdays after school, the teacher arranged a beautiful still life. She placed a pewter vase containing a spray of purple heather against a background of softly draped cloth. Most of the children had been coming to the class for some time and needed little introduction for the task, setting to like old hands. Although the subject was the same for all on this occasion, the paintings, as is usually the case, were as different as the children. One began with the background, using bold strokes, another with the vase in precise detail, others with the spray of heather. One girl of eight or nine finished off her gay version and did two other "free choice" paintings: her impression of an acrobat at the circus she had seen the week before, and, finally, a portrait of herself with a broad grin and feet firmly planted on a base line. When this was finished, she looked around the room in some surprise. "You still working on your *first*? I've done three!" No one seemed the least antagonized by her remark. These children seemed not only to know that they were accepted by their teacher, but how to accept each other, even in those moments of proud achievement that can so easily annoy and divide. Perhaps it was easy to accept this child because she had accepted herself, and could discover her abilities without boasting.

It is said that whenever St. Francis looked into the face of another human being, that person felt he was being valued and taken seriously. Even birds and animals felt secure in his presence, and he called the sun and moon his brother and sister. So close was his fellowship with God that he saw God reflected in things and animals as well as people. Paul Tournier says that poetry is an engagement of the self toward things, and that art and true religion also have this quality. In fact, he says, everything we encounter takes on the tone quality of thing or person depending on whether we ourselves are a thing or a person in respect to it. "When our eyes are opened to the world of persons, things themselves become personal." [2]

We respect the paintings of children because they are their personal work, and we begin to see that painting is much more than a mechanical gadget to keep children busy so as to be easier to handle. Anyone who will take the trouble to engage himself and his group seriously with painting will find it is an amazing instrument of amazing grace.

Take the instance of Timothy. If a miracle is something that cannot happen until it does, then Timothy's painting might be called a miracle, for his growth at one point seemed as sudden and dramatic a gift of grace as the conversion of St. Paul on the road to Damascus. Until the day of the "blood bath," as someone called it, Timothy had been painting along with the others in his group, but he gave the impression of not being very much "with it." He was an intelligent and likable boy, a delight to have in the class, but some of his work looked more like mud than anything else, even though all around him others were choosing colors that fairly sang. Then suddenly one day Timothy thrust his hands into a dish of red paint and splashed it gleefully up to his elbows. If some other child had done this, disciplinary measures might have been in order, but the teacher knew Timothy well and did not rebuke him. A few moments later he began to paint, and at the end of the hour he had completed a vigorous and colorful landscape, a veritable song of praise. It was as though the breath of life he had been given from the beginning now filled his being and stood him on his feet.

All that he said in words was, "This is a lot of trees, and this is the sky and the heavens," but together with his painting they were eloquent. One is reminded of the eighth Psalm:

> When I look at thy heavens, the work of thy fingers,
>   the moon and the stars which thou hast established;
> what is man that thou art mindful of him,
>   and the son of man that thou dost care for him?
> Yet thou hast made him little less than God,
>   and dost crown him with glory and honor.
>
> *Psalm 8:3-5*

It is only in knowing how it feels to be accepted as a person by another person that one can come to know the love of God. We expect teachers in the church school to accept differences in clothing, manners, language, and color, but we need also to consider how to accept the deeper differences in ways of thinking and feeling and behaving that come from various levels of culture, religious concepts, standards of value, and even from personality disturbance.

Because painting, when wisely conducted, is so individualized an activity, it has the power to reveal those kinds of differences and to give teachers a key to that deeper level of acceptance that every child must have before he can understand what Jesus meant when he prayed "Our Father." If a child knows this, he can move on to further insight when he hears the story of Jesus' baptism. When Ellen painted her version of this event she said, "The dove is coming down to the river Jordan to show that God has *accepted* his Son." So too, when a child can enter into that part of Jesus' life, he will understand and express more fully the meaning of Gethsemane, when Jesus is enabled to accept God's will for him in spite of the cost. Acceptance is a two-way street, but we cannot expect children to "accept Christ" meaningfully as teenagers if, as young children, they never knew what it is to be accepted themselves. They may say the words, but there will be no music accompanying them.

CHAPTER **3**

FOR GROWTH
AND UNDERSTANDING

Between the years of six and twelve, the life of a child expands mentally and spiritually as well as physically. He needs help to express this enlarging experience, both for his own understanding and to facilitate communication with others. Significant new ideas, feelings, and happenings are never really complete and never understood or appropriated until they are expressed in some way, and words alone cannot bear the entire burden of this necessary process. There are not enough ears to go around either at home or at school, and even if there were, children require a variety of expression to mature. They are born with the capacity to express themselves visually as well as verbally, and this makes painting a natural and desirable complement to speech for self-disclosure and communication.

According to Susanne K. Langer,[1] it is the power of speech that sets man above the animals, but the use of symbols in painting is also a kind of language. She says, "The symbol-making function is one of man's primary activities, like eating, looking, or moving about. It is the fundamental process of his mind, and goes on all the time. Sometimes we are aware of it, sometimes we merely find its results, and realize that certain experiences have passed through our brains and have been digested there."

Through our ability to create expressive symbols therefore, we can "relate ourselves meaningfully to other human beings and to the world around us." This symbol-making process, along with growth and understanding, is related to a timetable for physical development. The details vary with individuals, but everyone is influenced by the schedule. We can try to ignore it or hurry it along, but the better part of wisdom is to cooperate with it as we seek to help children understand and develop the concepts of the Christian faith. It is not the purpose of this chapter to explore the developmental stages of childhood except as they relate to the personal growth of children through the creative act of painting and its relevance to religious understanding. It is hoped, however, that the guidelines in the following pages will help church school teachers understand more of what they see and hear as they work with children in this field, for children surely need that kind of understanding as they try to bring order out of the confusing circumstances of their existence.

From the early scribbling common among preschool children to the more realistic work of junior highs, children pass through several transitions. The exact age at which these transitions occur cannot be predetermined, but they do occur in predictable patterns. The time when a child abandons one level of painting for another more advanced level varies with each child; and even after he has made a transition, he may revert under stress to an earlier period for a time.

It is generally accepted that all children's paintings mean something to them whether we can construe the meaning or not. Daniel Mendelowitz says that the way a child paints is an expression of what he understands, and what he paints is a direct expression of his interests. He goes on to say that each has his own style and that choice of subject matter and kinds of lines and colors are outgrowths of a child's experiences, physical make-up, and personality structure. The paintings appear haphazard and lack meaning only when we have not learned to "read" them.[2] The preschool child, for example, as he scribbles apparently meaningless marks on the paper, is not just wasting time. He is quite likely enjoying the physical motion over which later he will seek to exert conscious control until some sort of form begins to take shape. He may choose favorite colors to make "mass" paintings and can often tell in detail what these mean to him, although they are not likely to resemble what he is thinking in any way that an adult would recognize. He paints *meanings,* not *appearances.* Alschuler and Hattwick, in *Painting and Personality,* mention that two days before a baby was born to one family, the preschool daughter drew a face with crying eyes (her own), and that a child with a defective foot painted a self-portrait with extra legs on that side of the body.

Then, sometime between four and seven, a child comes into the symbolic period when he begins to be interested in a relationship between his thoughts and the objects around him. He discovers he can make something on paper which stands for these, and resembles them enough for adults to recognize. The first attempt at such a symbol may be a human figure, portrayed with a circular shape for the head and two lines for legs with or without loops at the end for feet. Lines for arms may appear next, possibly with five smaller lines for fingers. Next a hat, with hair usually appearing after that. Ears may be shown, at first, on each side near the top of the head. Details of clothing to distinguish between boy and girl figures are a still later development. Buttons usually show up when a child is learning to use them. Early tree symbols are often a circular shape resting on a vertical support (sometimes called the "ice cream cone" symbol, although this term is for the teacher's convenience only, since the symbol occurs among children who have never seen an ice cream cone). The symbolic styles chosen by children during this period are sometimes referred to as "modes" or "schemes." An interesting method often resorted to is the "x-ray," whereby a child paints both the outside of a house and what is inside it. He paints what he thinks of as "there," not what could actually be seen from the outside.

At this age, the size of the objects shown will often be in

proportion to their importance to the child, not to other objects in the picture. If a child has been helping his father rake leaves, he may paint himself with very big or very long arms, because they were the most important part of himself in that activity. If a child feels small and insignificant, he may paint himself very tall to compensate; if his home is of the utmost importance to him, he may fill most of his space with a house, leaving little room for other objects; if his father or mother mean more to him than anything else, he may portray a smaller house and a large man or woman figure towering above it. It would only puzzle him to suggest that he make his arms in proportion to the rest of his body, or his parents in proportion to the house, for that is not the criterion of size by which he is operating. That kind of standard will be meaningful to him later, but it is not now. A story is told of a mother who was trying to lose weight. She resented her young son's family portraits because he always showed her figure larger than that of any other figures in the group. Had she understood that this was his way of saying that to him she was the most important member of the family, she could have accepted the honor, instead of resenting the "insult." Ruth Mock tells a similar story about the lack of understanding shown by a teacher in England for a young boy's painting of a wicket-keeper in cricket. The teacher had explained *his* idea of a wicket-keeper as being tense and angular, but a nine-year-old had painted him broad and stolid. The boy had been awed by the keeper's "nothing-shall-pass-me" attitude, but the teacher was annoyed because he thought the child had not been listening.[3]

As a child progresses in experience, his paintings will reflect the changes within him. At first the child of four to seven paints his objects more or less scattered about the paper. Then, sometime during these years, he will begin to show a strip at the top for sky and another at the bottom for earth. Some objects will now be rooted firmly to the ground line, others may remain scattered about as before. The sun appears at this time in almost every picture, usually in one of the upper corners.

Often it is only half visible, the other half being imagined, off the paper. In between the sky and earth strips, the paper is left blank, as though reserved for the air. Some children become aware sooner than others of the horizon line, where sky and earth meet with no space left for air. Clouds, birds, stars, a moon may be added or substituted for the sun formerly alone in all its glory.

Children will grow more satisfactorily into the next level of expression if they are allowed to proceed at their own speed without being confused by standards for which they are not ready. When it is right for them, they will move to the next level. When one child moves faster than another, it is because of natural, individual differences, not because an overly ambitious adult, or one not knowledgeable about children, has tried to push him beyond his present level of performance. In fact, pressuring a child can hold him back.

In the case of seven-year-old Matthew, it was his mother who held him back by demanding adult behavior. On rainy days and weekends she gave him coloring books to fill in "with neatness and dispatch" and became so proud of his precision with crayons that she rewarded him with a painting kit for his birthday. It included tiny brushes, outline landscapes, and full directions as to where to place each color. She praised Matthew to the neighbors, too, and then wondered why he began to spill his milk at meals and drop his games with a noisy clatter. Then one Sunday morning at church school, Matthew's class had a painting session. When his mother called for Matt, she was shocked to see what he had been doing. Such big blobs of paint, such bright colors, and she couldn't even GUESS what the painting was meant to be. Matthew never did such untidy work at home! Why had he been such a bad boy today? It was not easy to help her, and it took a long time. Perhaps she never did fully understand that her son was painting younger than his age at church because he had been made to paint older than his age at home, and that if allowed to be himself, he might in time catch up with his own true level of behavior somewhere between these two unnatural extremes.

From ten to twelve, children approach adolescence with varying degrees of speed in a period sometimes called "latent," meaning hidden or dormant in contrast to the teen-age explosion. Although activity is not frenetic, it most certainly is not absent. Children come closer to realism in their art as the size and proportion of the objects they draw become more accurate, and as the objects are related to a ground "plane" instead of a ground "line." Perspective, which may have been taken up earlier and abandoned, is now inquired into more seriously. The development taking place in small muscles leads to more interest in precision and detail. This is a time when girls enjoy drawing figures with elaborate costumes, and boys turn to sketching planes, boats, and bridges. Although still children, they are more critical and less free, so concerned that everything be "just right" that they easily become discouraged. Wanting approval, some children will conform to popular standards to the extent of copying conventional art. Some will lose all spontaneity during this period. Still others, for a variety of reasons, will continue to maintain contact with their personal selves even while focusing their attention outward to their objective world.

It is vital that church school teachers keep in close touch and try to understand the underlying restlessness and uncertainty of these children. Painting can help because it offers an acceptable way to express thoughts and feelings without criticism, and because it provides subject matter that transcends banality and can keep imagination alive and robust. Important allies in the situation are the children's enthusiasm, strong sense of fair play, and the more lively interest in both intellectual and group activity which comes in this period. In art these can be channeled toward committee research, perhaps for background material for a classroom mural or settings for a puppet play; sharing an exhibit as a service project for a hospital, or a home for orphans or the aged; making posters for a mission project or a Youth Budget; illustrating Bible stories or hymns. Nevertheless, there should still be an occasional opportunity to paint for the joy of creating something beautiful out of their life adventure, whether it has a utilitarian purpose or not. In all that goes on, the wise teacher will offer encouragement, but when she gives praise it must be honest, or it will do more harm than good. As children become self-critical, they will appreciate constructive suggestions more than gushing insincerity, no matter how well-intentioned, and in the long run their sense of fair play will respond to integrity more wholeheartedly than to flattery.

During a conversation while traveling in America, the Hungarian composer Zoltan Kodály stated his belief in the interrelatedness of human abilities. His theories of education as well as his music have revolutionized some of the schools in Hungary. Through his influence, 103 out of the 6,000 schools now have singing every day, and in those schools, it is claimed, the pupils learn all their studies more easily. "Why not?" the composer said. "The voice sits in the body. To sing is to stimulate the body, and through the emotion, the mind."

It is quite probable that painting could be shown to have the same effect. At least the story of Tadao suggests this. He is a Japanese boy who was enrolled in a primary class in the middle of the school year. Other members of the class knew each other well, and Tadao was the only stranger in the group. Although he appeared to understand some English, he either did not know the language well enough to reply or was fearful of making a mistake. The teacher was concerned lest he continue to feel an outsider during the entire period of learning a second language.

Then one day when painting was included in the schedule, she discovered it could be at least one step in the solution of Tadao's problem, for there is no language barrier in painting, and Tadao was eloquent in that medium. His picture of a Japanese scene told his American friends something of his former life that he could not say in words. When on another day he painted the stately spire of his American church, it was as though he were saying, "Look, I feel more at home now." Interestingly enough, this second painting was more natural and childlike than the Japanese scene, and had more color and movement. The teacher thought that Tadao's English improved more rapidly after that, possibly because his confidence had been bolstered and his perceptions sharpened. Learning to organize objects on a page requires solving problems of related-ness, and who knows how much this may have helped. Perhaps it can also improve a child's ability to read.

We have already spoken in previous pages of paintings re-lated to God as Creator. God as a friend and helper is less readily perceived by children who are more accustomed to thinking of him as an awesome power far removed from us "down here below." We recall a painting of the Prodigal Son done by a nine-year-old girl who lives in a deprived area. She showed God giving advice to the Prodigal Son, but he was sitting on a cloud in the opposite corner from the young man. Although children may picture God guiding from a distance, they do not seem to doubt his power to do so. God was on the cloud, but the Prodigal Son had turned around and was on his way home.

Another expression of God's practical leadership was painted by a girl of seven who chose the moment when God commanded Moses to stop standing still. "Why do you cry to me? Tell the people of Israel to go forward." And forward they went. It was a moving little scene: Moses with his staff, the pillar of fire overhead, and the people holding each other by the hand, striding bravely into their frightening venture. "The people followed God's light," said the child, "and that is how they got across the desert." The young artist is a Negro, which may help to explain why she chose courage in a crisis and faith in God as the essence of her work, and why she stated it so clearly. It should be said here that no assignment was made to "paint a picture illustrating the idea of God as guide." The story was vividly presented, and the children had the privi-lege of responding each in his own way. Had it been otherwise, the experience might have been less rewarding.

Sometimes the crucial need for help in developing a true

rather than a false idea of God is revealed while a painting is in progress. An example of this occurred in an older junior group after a study of the prophet Amos. Various versions were made of Amos' warning to the people and what would happen if they did not repent of their injustice to each other. One child showed forbidding heavens with a darkened sun, another a bright blue sky over which a black cloud was moving toward the sun. But a third painted a giant, shadowy figure in gloomy tones of red and black hovering over a house in menacing attitude. It was the child's comment that helped the teacher see that she was probably confused in her thinking and feeling. "This is God, and he is warning the people." While the emphasis in the other pictures was on the prophet's warning of the results of human sin, here God himself was portrayed as fearsome and hostile. Conversation on the spot about the nature of God was crucial, and it is hoped that the child was helped to realize God is never against people, although his judgment is always opposed to their wrongdoing.

Another junior girl, a year or two younger, envisioned God not as being outside the moment of judgment, but within it. The motivation had been a deeply moving reading of Psalm 46:

> God is our refuge and strength,
>   a very present help in trouble.
> Therefore we will not fear though the earth should change,
>   though the mountains shake in the heart of the sea;
> though its waters roar and foam,
>   though the mountains tremble with its tumult.

> "Be still, and know that I am God.
>   I am exalted among the nations,
>   I am exalted in the earth!"
> The LORD of hosts is with us;
>   the God of Jacob is our refuge.

Psalm 46:1-3; 10-11

Being "still" and "knowing" had become so meaningful to Marjorie during the reading that she was able to paint clearly and with beauty the contrast between confusion and peace. At the heart of a whirling turmoil of muted color was the tiny figure of a man surrounded with a clear blue circle of calm. In the upper right-hand corner was another small figure, an angel with a trumpet. Marjorie's words were: "Everything is in chaos. It is the world's end, and Gabriel blows his horn. But in the midst of the worst is peace. God is there."

The idea of divine-human companionship comes most easily to children through stories of Jesus blessing the children, healing the blind, stilling the storm, or discovering Zacchaeus up in the tree. All these are popular with children because they are dramatic and intensely personal. Action and strong feeling stimulate good painting and, with transcendent content, help to establish personal understanding. These stories, and others that show the essence of Jesus as a person, we dare not let our children miss in this age of depersonalization. As Martin Niemöller said in a sermon preached in the United States, it would mean the "grave of human confidence and the grave of human hope."

Yet responses even to these stories can be both disappointing and puzzling. There was Peter, a boy of six who lived in a wealthy suburb. He had heard the story of the children gathered close around Jesus' knee, and had sung the song, including the words, "I love them and they love me." But in his painting, Jesus and the children were not close at all. Jesus was perched high above them on a thronelike chair. The teacher felt that the intellectual content of the picture was frightening, as though the children were slaves at his feet. The teacher may have been right, but recalling the need to reserve judgment, we must also look at other factors, such as the child's age. At six, children are not likely to relate objects to each other according to space, but according to their significance. The high throne may not have meant a distant Jesus, but a very important one.

Some of these differing images may come as a shock to teachers who think that children will understand the stories exactly as they themselves do. A teacher in Washington, D.C., discovered to her chagrin that her children had mistaken a presentation of David's procession with the ark of the covenant at Jerusalem for the President's inaugural parade. In another city, a boy just under six painted a picture of "Jesus" which looked like a monster in a gas mask, and a picture of "God" that resembled Mickey Mouse. There is a concept chasm in our Sunday morning schools not always based on segregation or poverty. If a child's work reveals consistent evidence of distress, a staff study of him, as seen through his visual expressions, may be in order. The study in turn should lead to a more adequate meeting of the children's needs in the entire church. Undoubtedly such a study would clarify the concepts of the teachers themselves and give more substance to their teaching as well as their faith. It could lead to the kind of teaching that involves exploring large ideas with children rather than learning sets of answers prescribed as correct. Through painting, we can discover the real thinking of children, how shallow our understanding of them often is, and what direction our teaching needs to take. A consultant in art can be helpful in this area, especially if she works with the minister. Finding such a person is not out of the question if there is a professional teacher in the congregation or a mother with art training who could catch the vision and volunteer.

A word must be said here about the kind of staff studies mentioned above. Let us not forget in our zeal for improving methods that our basic concern is with children who are alive and human and vulnerable. Let us not puff ourselves up with much learning and reject them ever so subtly for their "faulty" images. Perhaps what looks to us like a "monster in a gas mask" was intended to be a spaceman in a helmet, the nearest thing to Jesus the little boy could think of. We must love children with a creative love, knowing that God is greater than Mickey Mouse and can help both parents and teachers open doors to something new and good for all children.

"Teaching religious concepts" is in some sense a handy textbook term for something that is much more profound. Our mission as teachers in the Church is more like that of Israel: to "prepare a highway for the Lord." We try to make the "rough places a plain," not merely to instill an idea *about* God, but so that children may indeed come to know him. What is God like? We can say he is revealed in creation, holiness, obedience, judgment, forgiveness, and love, but because abstractions cannot stand alone in matters of faith, we tell stories that focus on specific people and events and that reveal God's nature. Instead of merely saying "God is holy," we tell the story of Isaiah in the Temple and let them discover God's holiness for themselves. As they make their own response through painting, they engage in a personal transaction not possible when sitting passively, taking our word for it.

". . . I saw the Lord sitting upon a throne, high and lifted up. . . . Holy, holy, holy! the whole earth is full of his glory. And the foundations of the thresholds shook . . . and the house was filled with smoke. And I said: 'Woe is me! For I am lost; for I am a man of unclean lips . . . for my eyes have seen the King, the LORD of hosts!' Then flew one of the seraphim to me, having in his hand a burning coal . . . from the altar. And he touched my mouth, and said: 'Behold . . . your sin is forgiven.' And I heard the voice of the Lord saying, 'Whom shall I send, and who will go for us?' Then I said, 'Here I am! Send me.' "

Isaiah 6:1-8

Prescott, a boy of eleven who usually painted with a rich variety of colors, gave the entire space in his Isaiah painting to the smoke swirling above the altar fire. This single-mindedness in gray and white represented for him an uncommon discipline. A golden flame and a few glimpses of black were the only contrast. On this one day he used a ruler in his work. "Because," he said in answer to a question, "this is the altar, and I want to be sure it's straight." When he had completed his work he made his final verbal statement: "In the center we have the white smoke because it has just come out of the altar and therefore is more pure. As it spreads, it thins and becomes more impure." In his portrayal of a spiritual experience, Prescott achieved an expression of beauty and strength as well as mystery.

Being related to the Church is in itself an avenue to a child's knowledge of God. There was special rejoicing when, over a period of two years, a junior girl had grown so much in her ability to speak through painting that by common consent her picture was given a place of honor at a closing exhibition. Light was streaming through the open door of the church, and in front of it was a tree shaped like a chalice. The verse chosen to accompany the painting was Exodus 25:8: ". . . let them make me a sanctuary, that I may dwell in their midst."

A skillful teacher has said that when children paint from the inside out, they may say things about their work that will embarrass them or take them by surprise. Ideas welling up freely from the deeper levels below conscious thought are scarcely recognized as their own, and they may giggle nervously or stand in awe. This happened one day when Wilhemina outdid herself. She was a shy child and, like many others of her age, somewhat inarticulate. When she first began to paint with other juniors at her church, she had had little previous experience in art, and her first work was rather dull. It was not long, however, before she began to catch the enthusiasm of the group and to enter with increasing interest into the tryout period when she could experiment with mixing colors and with different ways of putting paint on paper. It was during one of these explorations that she discovered the fun of dripping paint from a full brush to the paper below. Then one day the children were asked to portray something full of wonder for which they were deeply thankful. The idea caught on quickly, and in hushed concentration the children proceeded with their "wonder paintings." All the results were interesting, but Wilhemina's was astonishing. She had covered her paper with a deep black wash, and when it was dry, spattered white paint over it in a profusion of "planets and stars." Without a set pattern, she had created an impression of the heavens at night which suggested the vast mystery of space with infinite unseen reaches far beyond.

"It is the universe," she said slowly, "in which everything is." Then as if amazed at the strange quality of her own thought, she looked up with a question in her eyes, like a traveler feeling the way in a strange land. Had she sensed the possibility of a life without limitation, perhaps even without time?

CHAPTER **4**

FOR FELLOWSHIP

We know now that merely removing restrictions in the education of a child is not enough for his development toward creative maturity. The idea of natural unfoldment if limitations are removed has been found untrustworthy, for even though a child has a natural bent for meaning and communion with reality, "he cannot produce the content and the norms according to which he has to live, in which and through which alone he can become creative. . . ." [1] In other words, a child will not become a person in his own right automatically or in isolation.

In a book on the Biblical meaning of love, Reuel Howe has this to say: "God created man to live in relation with the world of things, with himself, and with his fellow men, and to live in these relationships in such a way that he will discover and grow in his relationship with God. . . ." [2] Howe goes on to describe the desperate feeling one has when shut out of an important relationship, how we lose our sense of well-being, begin to feel unwanted, less alive, but how we also can begin to know the joy of life once more when we are again gathered warmly in a group. "It is almost as though we had been resurrected. . . . The experience of fellowship makes the difference between life and death."

42

In a church school class, fellowship begins as anywhere else with the simple process of getting acquainted. On the first day, a child learns his teacher's name and she learns his, and gradually classmates begin to recognize each other not only by name but by appearance and behavior. The more a child participates, the sooner he will feel that he belongs. An amusing and encouraging exception to this "rule" occurred in a downtown church on a Sunday morning when Billy, whose mother taught the four-year-olds, was promoted to the "fives." When he arrived he remained standing near the door, aloof, but surveying the room with evident interest. On being invited to take part in the game, he shook his head. "I'm a new boy today, so I just watch. My mother says that's the way it goes. Next week I'll join the group."

Fellowship begins with recognition and moves toward mutuality through communication. One speaks to someone, someone answers. One takes hold of his partner's hand in a game and feels the warmth of his touch; a teacher starts a familiar song, the children sing it with her; she tells a story, conversation follows. For some this process will not be as easy as for others. If there has been no custom of talking things over at home, no real parental counsel, and hence no response, it will be difficult to draw these children into even an elemental sort of fellowship. The restlessness so noticeable in many classrooms today stems in large part from the children's having no relation to the source of life. It is not that they have "turned away from God" in willful pride, but that they have never had the privilege of encountering him. The kind of family life the Bible refers to as the answer for the "solitary" has become increasingly rare. Forty years ago it was considered shocking that 10 per cent of marriages in the United States ended in divorce. Now the rate is more than three times that, between 30 and 40 per cent. The effects of this deterioration of family life are seen not only in the public schools but in the Sunday morning church schools as well, even in so-called "good neighborhoods." An experienced supervisor using her "third ear" can determine with reasonable accuracy which classes have the largest proportion of children from broken homes. Voices are shrill, behavior is restless, the span of attention is short, and during a story or discussion some children find it difficult if not impossible to listen at all. Even if they are outwardly quiet, they may not be hearing a word, but merely keeping still with deaf ears to avoid antagonizing the teacher. They have tuned out their ears at home to protect themselves from unwelcome sounds, and it is not easy to tune them back in again.

Homes where both parents are living under the same roof may be just as truly broken as those where one parent is missing, in some cases more so. The lack of genuine love-in-relationship is inevitably reflected in the child, and the emptiness will make itself felt in ways that not only distress him, but his teacher and his classmates too. He may be shy and self-protective, fearful of making mistakes, or even hostile to a personal exchange. He may not even have the vocabulary with which to participate in it. The language of creative expression is important to all children, but for a spiritual orphan it is indeed a godsend, taking off the pressure caused by his inability to respond with the expected words or actions, giving him an opportunity to find his place in what may be the only possible way that exists for him in the beginning. "I can't tell you in words," one child said to his teacher, "but I can paint it for you." A child in such a predicament may welcome painting at an easel by himself, if one is available. Then, as he gains confidence, he can join the others in their work at the tables or on the floor. When acceptance and understanding tell him at last that he is loved, then he can safely mingle with his classmates, eventually to give as well as to receive. "We love, because he first loved us." (1 John 4:19)

A poignant illustration of the lostness of a child without love will underscore the need for adequate understanding and action on the part of the Church. Several years ago a child of European parents who had separated began turning up at the parish house on Sunday morning an hour before time for classes. Her presence there was not discovered until early one morning the superintendent heard mysterious footsteps on the second floor and went to investigate. There was little Sophie moving aimlessly from room to room in search of the Way, with no language but her search. There was no provision at that time for presession activity, but the superintendent did his best with picture books and did not send her away. Later, through pastoral help, the home was restored, and Sophie stopped coming early. The lost sheep was found, Jesus' parable re-enacted in modern dress.

It is experiences such as this that can lead a church school staff to establish an extended session. Many patterns are possible, ranging from a voluntary half hour before the regular period when at least a few teachers are present and the children can use materials for creative expression. Experiments can be tried until the one right answer for any given situation is found. In any case, it is the responsibility of the church to provide, along with the words and the concepts of faith, the experiences that make those words and concepts meaningful. A child who knows the fellowship of trust at home and on Sunday morning will be able to accept the idea of trust in God and to experience the reality of that trust in person.

This comes about through good teaching in a wide variety of ways, but how it happens at the church through painting is what we are concerned with here. When children know they are accepted, they are free to enjoy painting, and especially are they free to enjoy it in the company of others who are doing the same thing. It is an interesting paradox that individual values may be expressed more fruitfully in a group, provided the members have a common interest. This was magnificently illustrated one night in a telecast called "Simple Gifts." People who believe passionately in the rediscovery of joy through individual values, as opposed to those of mass production, were shown engaged in sailing, mountain climbing, collecting antiques, and so on. The mountain climber was always taking friends up with her to share the adventure and the view. The collectors swarmed to a sale where they met other collectors.

The sailor refused to "use" his hobby as a means of retreat, preferring it as a direct experience of communication with his boat, the sea, and his two sons, who came along to learn the same kind of values.

The enjoyment that comes to children when they work in a group meets two needs: the need to have respect for themselves and the need for fellowship with others. Without relatedness, self-respect becomes self-centered, and without individual values, a group can become a lonely, uncreative crowd. What kind of group it will be depends to a large extent on the teacher. If she can resist the temptation to hover over her pupils while they work, attempting to impose her ideas on them, and can instead release them to freedom in fellowship rather than isolation, she can do much to supply the two needs mentioned above. The children can then move away from imitating others to original creation.

Fellowship is felt both in the spirit of the room and in special happenings, either incidental or planned. At a show-and-tell time, when the children bring their finished work to a circle to share with each other, appreciation is both given and received. One Sunday morning after a group of children had been making pictures while listening to a recording of the hymn, "This Is My Father's World," one little girl was asked by her neighbor to explain the meaning of a five-pronged shape with an "egg" in the center. "That's the hand of God," she explained, "and the thing in the middle is the world. He's holding it."

During clean-up time precious moments of conversation are possible for the teacher and those who have volunteered to help. Personal opinions and news of life at home can be exchanged as in a family kitchen while the dishes are being washed. Some of the deepest levels of fellowship, however, must be carefully planned for, as at Christmas when the Advent paintings have been completed. One such time stands out especially. Children in an after-school group at church were invited a week in advance to plan on staying overtime the following session for a party. After class the leaders brought out frosted cookies and ice cream as the children helped to push the tables into one long board that would include everyone. Lights were turned off, the teacher lighted a tall taper, and heads were bowed for grace. Into that moment all the Friday afternoons of the last two months were poured and lifted up. Each had come to know so much more than the names and faces of their friends around the table; they had come to know each other's thoughts and feelings, something of their very lives, as they had painted in each other's company their personal responses to the most joyous story ever told. They had learned that good painting grows from the inside out and also, in some measure perhaps, that art is man's expression of himself, his world, and his faith. As the candle glowed and grace was said, the Light of the world was most wondrously present. The good news had been proclaimed and heard, and members of the class were united in deep fellowship. As good-bys were said, the teacher gave each child a tiny Japanese bell in token of other children in other lands, for joy must not be hoarded among ourselves.

Although the Christmas story is indeed a special one to help children know the truth of divine-human dialogue, there are many others in the Bible appropriate for grades one through six. Moses and the Burning Bush is a favorite with primaries, and Mount Sinai is popular with both primary and junior children, who enjoy portraying the lightning on the mountaintop as God spoke to Moses, or the people at the foot waiting to respond to God's offer of a covenant relationship.

Harriet was only eight when, in painting her own interpretation of the events in Exodus 19, she departed from her customary style of trees and flowers under a sunny sky. The story must have made an unusual impression, for her mountain and the people at the foot were alike involved in an awesome event. Sinai was shown as a pinnacle of rock, sturdy, but shaken by tremors and shrouded in smoke, with a "blazing" fire at the summit. Even though, as Harriet explained, the "blueness of the sky shows through," the people below seemed to be gazing upward in awe, or turning away as if to escape. Harriet must have heard a new note in depth as the story unfolded that day, for her painting had power in color and movement and was a dynamic representation for her age of the covenant between man and God.

As an approach to the meaning of Easter, one teacher gave a unique assignment to a class of younger juniors who had just ended a review of the entire life of Christ. She asked the children to choose one story to paint from, and to choose only one detail by which to represent the meaning of that story. For a change she provided construction paper in a wide choice of colors instead of the usual manila, and partly because of this some children painted in outline with black poster paint. The results were interesting. One child chose the healing of the blind man as his story and, for the detail, a large pair of eyes slanted at an oblique angle across the paper. Another chose the Bethlehem skyline for the Nativity, a third, three crosses on a hill. Some thought the most meaningful picture was a rather crude bowl and pitcher representing Christ's washing of the disciples' feet, for this revealed him as servant as well as master. These pictures, when combined with the appropriate verses from the Bible and the events they brought to mind, provided a moving experience for the class as well as a summary of their review. Although the results were not paintings in the usual sense (being more like symbolic signs), neither were they stiff and impersonal. The children had managed to convey in their irregular lines and shapes something of themselves as well as of the meaning of the story.

The profound message of fellowship revealed in the events of Easter can be caught and expressed by children through painting and words far better than through painting or words alone. For example, older juniors especially appreciate knowing that the Lord's Supper not only shows God's concern for his people then and there in Jerusalem, but points back to his care at the time of the Passover in Egypt and forward to the importance of a life of communion through the Church. They can see that this final moment of fellowship before his betrayal deepens the meaning of servanthood revealed earlier in the washing of the disciples' feet. When the children know these things, and have discussed them, they will listen, quietly attentive, to the vital words read directly from the Bible. Then they are ready to paint: "And when the hour came, he sat at table, and the apostles with him. . . . And he took a cup, and when he had given thanks he said, 'Take this, and divide it among yourselves.' . . . And he took bread, and . . . broke it and gave it to them, saying, 'This is my body. But behold the hand of him who betrays me is with me on the table. . . . Let the greatest among you become as the youngest, and the leader as one who serves.' " (Luke 22:14-21)

Two examples of children's work on the theme of the Last Supper, done in churches many miles apart, will indicate their ability to paint meanings if they are deeply understood. Although both paintings are about the same subject, they are very differently expressed. The first, by a ten-year-old girl, is painted starkly, with a minimum of detail, yet there is an unmistakable sense of crucial happening. Thirteen figures are seated at the table, but Jesus is easily recognized by his attitude of humble devotion. His head is bowed, and the background is dominated by a cross. The child's comment completes our understanding of her intention: "This is the Last Supper, with the Cross in Jesus' mind. The disciples didn't know about the Cross yet."

The second is by a girl of eleven who concentrates her attention on Jesus and the meaning of a brilliant yellow background in relation to him. We see a "close-up" of Jesus facing us at table, and the presence of the disciples is merely suggested by circles representing plates. The table is not entirely shown, for it comes toward us off the paper, and the near end of it has to be imagined. This child has become interested in perspective, as the lines of the table indicate, and in spiritual meanings, as her comment shows: "The yellow-yellow and more yellow is the radiance. It is God with him. He is about to break the bread."

The events of Easter move swiftly through the climax of

the Crucifixion, which seems to shatter the basis of all true fellowship, to the final truth of the Resurrection, which re-affirms the good news of Christmas and the life of Jesus. Children's paintings of the Easter events continue to amaze us by their depth of insight into Biblical truth. A boy of eight shows three crosses in a dark setting of mysterious depth and gloom; a girl of eleven paints the curve of earth beneath the Cross to indicate that although the people at the foot are mocking Jesus, he is making his sacrifice not only for them but for the entire world; a boy of ten paints a dark sky and rocks crashing from a cliff into a raging sea to tell how the earth was shaken when Christ was crucified, then in a companion picture transforms the same setting into one of peace and promise, calling it "The Dawn of a New Day." At the time this painting was made, the boy's father had just come home from a term in jail for his part in one of the "freedom rides," an event that may have influenced the boy's interpretations.

The theology in children's painting may not always agree with our own, but instead of criticizing it, we can accept and enjoy it, knowing that the blade must come before the full ear of corn, and that the children are struggling to express their understanding of an Event whose meaning was beyond the comprehension of the disciples themselves. Life-and-death and life-after-death are big questions, and what children try to say about them we will most certainly want to hear even though we may not always understand their meaning. When a girl paints a picture of her grandmother's garden as she remembers it from a visit there on Easter, let us notice the clear bright colors which seem to tell of a happy memory; when a younger child paints two figures and says they represent "God helping my grandpa that died . . . in a rainbow and snow," we are enchanted by the charm of his concept even though we cannot tell which figure is God and which is Grandpa; when a boy chooses to paint his church "early one Easter morning," we may not know just what this means to him, but we appreciate his way of relating the Resurrection to his own life.

There is a painting by a girl of eleven which shows how conscious effort to understand increases during the preteen period: the empty tomb in the center is surrounded by flowers, and light comes from behind it as well as from within. She says, "This is just as the sun is rising on Easter morning. I show he wasn't there any more. He has risen. But his light is there." A fourth-grade girl portrays with tenderness the appearance of Jesus to Mary in the garden, and an older girl, the day of Pentecost, describing it poetically: "The wind blew and small flames danced as the Holy Spirit was given to the people." Bringing Pentecost straight into his own experience, a boy of twelve executed a design astonishing in its simplicity and meaning: the figure of a boy is standing in the center of a curved space from which lines radiate to the outer edges of the paper. "Sometimes I feel like love is radiating out of me," he said, "and I feel very warm."

No account of fellowship as experienced and interpreted by children is complete without illustrations of their art related to the Church. We have already referred to the joy with which a blind boy expressed in color an image of his church. His comment mentioned that the sky was "bluish-green," apparently a treasured memory from the days when he could see. A girl of six called her painting "Church with People Going," making her building gaily blue and yellow, with a bright red door, and perching it high up on a sort of pedestal in token of its importance. The picture is not only cheerful but well-balanced, with a boy and girl planted sturdily on each side. The girl is slightly larger than the boy and her clothes more colorful, leading one to guess that this may have been a portrait not only of her church but also of herself and younger brother on a Sunday morning. In another church a boy of the same age presented his picture very differently. He indicated the essential form of the church to be large and strong and bulky, with no upward movement in line or shape, but since the colors he used were gloriously warm, there is little doubt of how he felt.

Naturally the manner of painting will be influenced by the architecture of a church building as well as by the interest and perceptiveness of the child. A bell, a steeple, or a stained-glass window, an impressive tower, or just a simple cross over a battered door may appear in paintings depending on the circumstances. One sensitive boy of ten painted gray stone walls at the side of a pointed arch, then added lovely tones of blue "to show it is alive." To a nine-year-old girl who had learned that art is not photography, the important things to paint about her church were both realistic and imaginary. She studded a plain door with jewels, blithely created an orange sunset in the west and a forest of antennas bristling from surrounding roof tops. Since she made no comment, we cannot be sure whether or not she said what we would like to think she said, namely, that her church is beautiful and glorious, and does not live in isolation but in a neighborhood. A boy of nine in an all-Negro church showed appreciation as well as skill in his firm foundation with a strong upward thrust crowned by a cross. He chose refreshing tones of blue and violet, using yellow accents and brushing on the color with quick, sure strokes. In an academic community, a ten-year-old girl painted her church as she saw it through her window at night. "Everything seems to move around *it*," she explained with emphasis.

Sharing one's creative work with others is a crowning act of relationship. The simplest way, and except for a show-tell period the one most easily executed, is when the teacher puts the paintings up around the room. For our purposes, all the work should be chosen for this intimate sharing, not just a selected few. If there is a bulletin board in the corridor or in an entrance way, however, only the pictures that can best speak to children or adults as they come and go should be displayed. A hall is a happier place when children's paintings are on the walls, and those who help to put them there will not complain of the work involved when they see their friends pause to look and wonder.

In addition to these casual ways of letting pictures communicate with people and bring them together, specific events can be planned: perhaps a tea for both parents and children in a classroom at the end of a series, or a more extensive exhibit open to the congregation and their friends. If given a special invitation, day-school teachers and children's librarians will welcome the opportunity to see what children are doing in another context.

During a family camping experience, one church learned how pleasant it was for all ages to paint together on a rainy day. Later they tried painting on a bright day and liked that too, finding both merriment and respect as they discovered each other in new, astonishing ways. Some images of perfection came tumbling down and others were revised upward. Roles were reversed as children encouraged parents heretofore "deprived" of exposure to this kind of art. Painting is for all kinds of weather, for at Christmas this same group tried it again at a Family Workshop party, and when it came time for worship, the reading of the Christmas story spoke to hearts and minds more ready to receive it because they had been revealed creatively to each other first.

Paintings can also be shared in services of worship—informally during vacation school, more formally perhaps on Sunday morning. When parents come to a closing program in the summer, it is good to have the summer's art around the walls, and to join the children as they sing:

Praise to the Lord, the Almighty, the King of creation!
O my soul, praise him, for he is thy health and salvation!
All ye who hear, now to his temple draw near;
Join me in glad adoration! [3]

If a single painting is being considered for use in more formal worship, it is important that it have a universal quality rather than a merely personal meaning, or it will intrude on the children instead of speaking to them. In one church there was to be a special service for older children relating to the troubled events in the world. The painting based on Psalm 46 that was described in Chapter 3 had just been completed and seemed to fit the occasion perfectly. The girl who had painted it was willing to bring her work to worship and explain how she had tried to show in her picture what the Psalm meant to her: ". . . chaos, but in the midst of the worst is peace. God is there." At the end of the service a classmate came up to her and held out his hand. "Congratulations," he said, "your painting is beautiful." Perhaps he too had discovered in his own way the difference between confusion and the peace of God.

An inspiring project in fellowship through art has come to our attention, one sponsored by the Children's Work Committee of a major denomination.[4] Paintings by children all over the state were gathered in an exciting exhibit at Lewis and Clark College, where the writer had the privilege of viewing them. There were ninety paintings by children ranging in age from the preschool years through junior high, and the subject matter was related to religious themes similar to those adopted by the National Council of Churches: "the participant's understanding and feeling about God, Jesus Christ, the Bible, and the Church." At each age-level the pictures were fresh and original in approach, charming and sometimes beautiful in color and arrangement. One representing the journey of Mary and Joseph into Egypt could have been a Grant Wood country scene, except that it was lovelier! The story was Biblical, but the setting was not. Like painters of the Renaissance, this child had chosen the setting from her own familiar surroundings. Her road to Egypt wound through the rolling fields and orchards of lush Oregon, and the magnificence of the setting sun belonged to the Pacific coast rather than the valley of the River Nile.

Some of the paintings had a depth of meaning capable of challenging adults to rethink their Christian commitment. One such, entitled, "Amos Today," was of a tenement district, and another showed people turning their backs on a preaching prophet and walking away.

The fellowship generated by this project was not achieved by the exhibit alone. When the invitation was issued to the local churches, suggestions were made that in order to motivate the series of three or four painting sessions, parents and children should choose from a given list of subjects the one they wished to think about and discuss at home in preparation. Children from the homes that cooperated were therefore ready to begin when they arrived at the class on Saturday or after school. Parents were also given the opportunity to lead the actual session, which meant preparing the room and materials and being present but not, in most cases, actually doing any teaching. The work was to be entirely the children's own. Naturally this gave the parents a deep interest in what was going on and an insight into the thinking and feeling of their children. Following the central exhibit, others were planned for local areas, and twenty paintings were selected to form a permanent traveling exhibit for the state.

To carry on this kind of project, or to sustain the kind of teaching we have been describing, a teacher must be the kind of person who can continue to grow. We cannot ignore this need in ourselves if we are to provide the strength and the spirit that are required. Her own discoveries and experiences along this line have been expressed by Margaret Grimes Adams, Director of the YWCA at the University of Pittsburgh, in an unpublished paper from which the following brief summary is made with her permission. Borrowing from Thoreau, Mrs. Adams speaks of the need to have eyes and ears open to more than the visible, and she goes on to state that leaders must have time to mature in wonder and surprise and curiosity, to listen to music, to talk with friends, to be open and willing to accept criticism, either constructive or demonic. A leader also has a need to be alone at times, to recognize her own selfhood and the gifts in her own life as well as those of others:

gifts from which she can no longer run away. She must have love and acceptance for herself, too, the strength and support of being accepted as a companion, one of the group, for "only as I am confronted by others can I become a person . . . and participate in . . . communion."

Each one of us needs his communion with people and with God to function with children in fellowship. The chairman of a junior department learned this in a deeply moving way. She had met with the teachers during Lent so that they could think through together the meaning of Jesus' life and death and resurrection in their own lives. When she visited a fourth-grade class shortly after Easter and saw the Easter pictures the children had painted posted on the wall, she was pleased and wanted to let the children know how she felt. "What could be better!" she added, not meaning it as a question, when to her surprise one of the girls responded as if it had been. "I'll tell you what would be better," she said. "To have Jesus come here in person. They say he rose from the dead, but I don't see him around!" The class held its breath. The teacher looked at the visitor imploringly and the visitor, seeing that the child was serious, prayed for help. "Don't you know that he *is* here?" she asked finally.

"Where?" the child demanded. "Over there by the door?"

"No," said the visitor, "nearer than that."

"In that chair?" she asked, pointing to a vacant seat, mocking.

"No, even nearer than that!"

The silence was electric as the girl kept her eyes on the visitor's face. Suddenly several children began to speak at once: "He's here . . . in our hearts . . . with all of us."

"Yes," said the visitor. "That is our Easter faith. He said he would be with us always, and we believe he is. Nearer than our hands and feet. Nearer than breathing."

She turned to go, but the child followed her to the door.

"Stay with us," she said, taking hold of the woman's hand. "Stay and talk with us some more."

Both children and adults can meet the risen Christ in the fellowship of the Holy Spirit, a fellowship in which, regardless of age, we are open to each other as persons. If we adults were better prepared, and our faith more confident and expectant, these moments of meeting would not come so infrequently, or as such a surprise, and we would all participate more abundantly in the work of Christ.

CHAPTER 5

FOR APPRECIATION

In its wider meaning, appreciation is an extension of fellowship, for we cannot have one without the other. When children are in fellowship with each other and their teacher, they are more likely to be appreciative than competitive. Instead of hearing, "Jan's painting is the best," followed by, "I don't buy that. Bill's is," followed by free-for-all argument that is meaningless, we are more likely to hear something like this: "How did you mix that shade of green?" "Just added more yellow." "Boy, you got a real neat palm tree there, but who's the guy under it?" "Can't you tell? That's Joseph." When pictures go up for display, naturally children will like some better than others, but they can learn that each person has a right to his own style, which may be just as "good" as the style somebody else likes better. If one child paints his church with slide-rule precision brick by brick, and another prefers a riotous abstract of many colors, that is their privilege, and children can learn to grant this to each other.

This attitude is also related to acceptance, although it may have the flavor of companionship and enjoyment rather than compassion and concern. Of course, one cannot isolate these attitudes as Benjamin Franklin tried to do in his essay on virtues, each to be developed on a certain day of the week. Our traits of character exist in one bundle, and our behavior is the result.

To keep our appreciation of children from being superficial, a growing foundation of knowledge and experience is necessary. It is not necessary, however, to know everything about art, the Bible, child psychology, and methods of teaching before we let painting introduce us to another way of knowing children. Whatever we do know can help if we keep it in perspective and remember that the primary requirement is to like children well enough to enter into their lives and spend some time there with open eyes, ears, mind, and heart. The rewards are great. We may have known our children by the color of their eyes, the way they walk and talk or answer questions, and whether they prefer apple juice or Hawaiian punch. Now we begin to discover whether they paint boldly or with hesitation, with pale colors or with bright, and whether they remember to wash their brush before putting it away!

Emily outlines her flowers in black, and perhaps we will never be sure why, but for the present this is part of Emily and endears her to us. We can't help being interested, however, if mannerisms are repeated, for a child's personality is always reflected in whatever he does. Because of this, painting can deepen the dimension of our acquaintance. Bill paints quickly, with pleasing colors; Charlotte chooses blue in various tints and shades, adding an ethereal "mist" of white. Jane uses earthy brown with a tang of orange; Marvin specializes in spectacular build-ups that take hours to dry. But here comes Leonard, making a maze of lines in an abstract design, but there is no confusion. He seems to know where he is going. Sally decorates everything she does with a row of small, bright flowers. Millicent likes action and paints her stories with a directness that does not puzzle the viewer. These clues are all more revealing than the modes or schemata discussed in Chapter 3, and the reason is that they are individual expressions rather than stages of growth typical of many children.

Viktor Lowenfeld writes in a fascinating way about line and color having a life of their own:

A line may be calm, like the horizontal line in a peaceful evening landscape; a line may be unpredictable, and excitingly change its direction like a lightning flash in a thunderstorm; a line may go busily from one point to another, as though its aims were predetermined; a line may go loafing around, as we do if we have nothing definite in mind. If one line meets another, it can be "angry" with it. . . . Two lines may also "walk together" in perfect harmony. Also, a color "may feel" fine or disgusted. . . . But red, just like you, can meet a friend. What color is a "friend" of red? Red can be in harmony with its friend or it can fight the friend. It can be triumphant and glorious, or can walk almost unrecognized in the "shadow" of the other colors. Such can be the life of colors. They do not need to represent "something." Like music, *they may have their own lives.*[1]

Lowenfeld goes on to say that when a child makes an abstract painting, he may not have any such thoughts about line or color in mind, but they will be present unconsciously, and, through experiments all the way from merely "dabbling" to conscious arranging and rearranging in various blobs and patterns, he can develop his own distinct expression and improve his ability to organize his work, "a part of the creative and investigatory spirit which is so vital for his future life." [2]

Children's work is often fanciful in spite of the current concentration on scientific interest in children's books. Librarians tell us that although fairy tales have been less popular than they were a generation ago, many children want their realism spiced with whimsical flights of fancy, as in the Mary Poppins books. This fascinating combination often appears in children's paintings of Biblical material. Zacchaeus has been seen perching in a bright red cherry tree instead of the sycamore provided in the story, and Noah's ark may look more like an oriental barge straight out of the Arabian Nights than the traditional image. These expressions should be appreciated as the child's privilege of artistic license.

Through the children's own painting, teachers have an opportunity to introduce an appreciation of the art of the masters. Art and religion both seek to reveal reality, and each can complement the other. Rufus Jones, writing of the beauty that is always breaking through in the world in ways both simple and sublime, must have understood something of the artist's vision when he called beauty a gift of sheer grace which must imply behind things a spirit that enjoys beauty for its own sake. Mr. Jones went on to say that whenever it can break through it does, and that our joy in it shows that we are in some sense kindred to the giver and revealer of it. Of course, it is not always beauty which art and religion seek to interpret. Evil and suffering are also a part of life, and contemporary artists try to deal with this in their own way. Picasso, in his painting "Guernica," comments on the horrors of war, Emil Nolde portrays a gaunt prophet agonized by what he understands. Although this kind of message through art is more appropriate for youth than children, older juniors can know that art has its crucifixion as well as its joy.

A natural opening for appreciating art may occur when a child's painting is seen to bear a resemblance to the work of a known artist, an exciting phenomenon that actually does take place, and not infrequently. The kneeling figure of Mary in an Annunciation scene painted by a fifth-grade girl may remind one of Mary's humility in a Florentine painting of the same subject; Mina's "Universe" is like a Jackson Pollock; Carmencita paints tulips with the same deep shades of red and blue that Nolde uses in his "Flowers"; Timothy's vigorous painting of a landscape, mentioned in Chapter 2, has something of the feeling in Rembrandt's etching called "Three Trees," which hangs at the E. B. Crocker Art Gallery in Sacramento; the black thunderclouds in an eight-year-old's picture of Jesus stilling the storm reminded a professional art teacher of the booming kettledrums in the storm movement of Beethoven's Sixth Symphony, an impression which Van Gogh could have appreciated, for he too recognized a relationship between art and music. Children should know about these affinities when they are present, for their sense of wonder keeps them humble, and they are seldom falsely proud of their creations. They will not overestimate their accomplishments if the teacher points out that all art has a language of its own, and children can speak it too. This in itself is a thrilling extension of fellowship across the barriers of time and age.

This revelation can happen also in a teacher's workshop, as it did in a group of forty women who were being trained to lead vacation schools in Manhattan. Three of their paintings on the Creation theme were found to be much like Paul Galdone's illustrations for *The First Seven Days*, a book for children based on Genesis, which none of them had ever seen. The book was brought to class the following day and everyone thoroughly enjoyed seeing the amazing similarities.

A portfolio of reproductions of great religious paintings is a helpful addition to a teacher's equipment. If the usual 25-cent size is too expensive for the church school budget, there are very good prints in post-card style for 10 cents each, although one must be willing to take the time to write various museums where they may be available. (See the list of museums in the Appendix.)

A word of caution is in order here. Prints of masterpieces should never be shown and discussed before the children have finished their own original version of the subject. We must not encourage them to imitate and lose their spontaneity. On the other hand, seeing the work of a master afterward can enrich a child's enjoyment without destroying his initiative. During the Advent Season, for example, when the painting sessions have been completed, children should see good reproductions of great Christmas art and talk about them together. What is the artist trying to say? Does he say it well? Do you like his color, the expression on the faces? How does the picture make you feel? Reverent, joyous, uplifted? What do you notice about the setting? Does it belong to Jesus' day, with the olive trees and dry stony ground of Palestine, or has the artist used his own time and place? Children might enjoy comparing a copy of Robert

Campin's "Annunciation," painted in Spain and showing the brass candlestick and kettle of a Spanish kitchen, with the same subject painted by the Flemish artist van der Weyden, showing a glimpse of a medieval castle through the open window. They could imagine how a city artist today might choose the terrace of his high-rise dwelling for the scene. Children will enjoy seeing *Away in a Manger*,[3] a charming little book of Christmas paintings as interpreted by children around the world. They all relate to the same good news, but each reveals something of its own distinctive national origin.

A gallery of great Madonnas could be hung in the hall for all to enjoy. Primary children can bring a favorite print for their Wonder Table, juniors for an easel or a bulletin board. Since children like making collections, they could develop their own gallery of post-card prints. If there is an art museum near enough to visit, going to it would be an inspiration at any time of year, but especially at Christmas. "For those who take the time to look at this art, and listen as did the shepherds of old, there may come again the message 'Glory to God in the highest, and on earth peace among men with whom he is pleased!' Art can help people even in troubled times to fix their eyes on the eternal." [4]

Such a visit should be carefully planned in advance if it is to help build a foundation for spiritual and artistic enrichment. This is important not just for the moment, but also for a child's future. Parents can be enlisted to help organize the trip and to accompany the children. If there is no civic museum, there may be a private gallery or a college art department which has a collection that could be opened to the children sometime during the year. There are also exhibits of children's paintings that spring up from time to time in various cities at the public library or at a museum. New York has one each year during Brotherhood Week that features paintings by children of many faiths, and another sponsored by the Police Athletic League.

A showing of art from the Immaculate Heart College in Los Angeles some years ago was inspiring to people of all ages because the "student investigations," as they were called, were unusually refreshing in their direct and free approach. Children of Sunday morning church schools will be especially interested in seeing an international children's exhibit sponsored by the World Council of Christian Education if it comes their way. In this collection the entries are all by children, and all are based on Biblical material. Paintings speak across barriers of race and creed, and children can learn to appreciate these voices especially when they understand their message.

Educators in the field of art now tend to think that talent is not a special endowment but a combination of factors such as the possession of good intelligence, genuine enjoyment of the medium and a drive to persist in it, plus the praise and encouragement of adults. This combination may not be nearly so rare as we used to think. Included in the combination, however, should be a perceptual awareness that enables a child to appreciate the world around him. For a number of reasons, many children in a city have a tendency to be blind to its beauty. We tend to downgrade the familiar whether we live in the city or the country, but there is among many in the city an attitude of resignation, one that accepts the fate that brings them to a dirty, noisy place away from open country or smaller towns. This is easy to understand, yet since three out of four people are either living in the city or about to, we must help our city children to be alive to the treasures all around them. There is real beauty in most cities, and some of it magnificently man made, as in bridges and buildings. But much of it is in people and what they are doing if only we have eyes to see and ears to hear.

One Sunday morning a young teacher who had recently come to a large city was so shocked by the cynical comments of his fourth-graders, when he asked them what they considered beautiful in their city, that he decided to do something about it. He recorded a tape of the noises under a busy bridge one rainy day and played it back for them the next week. First he described the bridge, how massive the supports, how graceful the curve of the arches overhead. Then he turned on the recording: horns tooting in different keys, wheels splashing in and out of puddles, the swish of tire treads, voices calling, trucks rumbling like thunder overhead, someone singing for a passing instant. It all made a montage of sound that surprised and fascinated the children, especially because they felt he had chosen such an unlikely spot for anything interesting. After that they began to be more aware of life around them. In fact it was this same class, already described in Chapter 1, that later asked if they could paint the joy of Easter. Perceptual development may have helped to sharpen spiritual awareness as well as the artistic.

From the fourth grade up there are any number of ways to help children do this. One could play a recording of "My Favorite Things" from *The Sound of Music* and let the children make up their own class list together, as the teacher writes their choices on the board. Or the class can take a "beauty walk," looking for leaves, geraniums in a window box, new arrangements in a florist's window, smoke rising from a chimney, the pattern of rain on a windowpane. Children can listen for the sound of laughter, the song of a bird, music through an open window. They can pretend they are a camera looking for a subject which expresses feeling, such as a child holding a puppy outside a supermarket or a tired old man resting on a curb. Children can keep their findings secret, if they wish, until they return to their room for a sharing time before they paint.

A class can go out in summer or winter and learn to see essential form, squinting their eyes and shutting out detail as they look at a tree or a building. Is the form tall and slim, low and sprawling, big and bulky, round, pointed? Then hurrying back, they paint quickly what they can remember. In the words of August Macke, a young German artist who was killed in France during the First World War, "To understand the language of form, is to come close to the mystery, to be more alive." [5] We need to learn how to look *into* things rather than at them. Going out to sketch can also sharpen observation. For children this should be kept very simple. They should use smallish sheets of paper clipped to cardboard and just one crayon apiece. In late fall, brown crayon on manila paper is effective for sketching bare trees, fences or stone walls, light posts, figures walking. In spring, green is good.

Practice in seeing the "living line" is helpful in developing a sensitive eye. One of the children can be asked to dance around to music (someone can sing if a piano or record player is not available) and to freeze in position when the music stops. Then everyone tries to catch the essential line of the figure very quickly without detail and without lifting the crayon from the paper. Presto, you're off for the next whirl, and it's time to try another drawing. If the teacher cannot sing, she can count from one to ten as in the game of "Statue." An objective experience such as this is a complement to children's imaginative painting, for it reminds them of the outer world which they must discover as well as the inner. Older juniors, especially, enjoy it because of their increasing interest in objective realism.

In talking of perceptual growth we need to remember that we can make it available to a child and lead him toward it, but that if its discovery is to be meaningful, he must make it himself. Nor will any particular discovery be exactly the same as that made by another child in the same circumstance. C. S. Lewis gives an account of an interesting experience from his own childhood. His family lived in the country near the sea and had a garden and a view of distant mountains, yet he had no knowledge of beauty until the day his brother brought home the lid of a biscuit tin which he had "covered with moss and garnished with twigs and flowers so as to make it a toy garden or a toy forest. That was the first beauty I ever knew. What the real garden had failed to do, the toy garden did. It made me aware of nature—not, indeed, as a storehouse of forms and colors but as something cool, dewy, fresh, exuberant. . . . As long as I live my imagination of Paradise will retain something of my brother's toy garden." [6]

It is evident that even the natural beauty of the countryside does not make awareness of beauty automatic. What parents hold dear will open some doors; others may remain closed until a new influence shows the way. "No picture on the walls of my father's house ever attracted—and indeed none deserved—our attention. We never saw a beautiful building nor imagined that a building could be beautiful," says Lewis.[7] He was the product, among other things, he says, of "endless books." "There were books in the study, books in the drawing room, books in the cloakroom, books (two deep) in the great bookcase on the landing, books in a bedroom, books piled as high as my shoulder in the cistern attic. . . ." [8] Although he does not say so, he must have received from those books a stimulus toward beauty in words whether he realized it at the time or not.

Far rarer today than family interest in natural beauty is a knowledge of the beauty to be found in the Bible. Those few children in Sunday morning schools who come already familiar with the Bible's rich heritage are able to put more meaning into their creative action than those whose minds and emotions are not so furnished and inspired. As a teacher explained in trying to account for the moving portrayal by a ten-year-old girl of Jesus' resurrection appearance to Mary, "As far as I know she has had no art instruction outside of regular church school and public school situations. However, she has a natural interest in art and in theology, and her home situation stimulates her development along these lines." Just how much interest in any given case is natural and how much the result of home influence is hard to say, but there is no doubt that the potential flame requires a spark from beyond itself before it can be activated.

One of the best resources from the Bible to extend children's knowledge of both beauty and religious devotion is the Book of Psalms. Used for over twenty centuries as a manual of public worship, this collection of poetry and song was the official hymnbook of the Temple at Jerusalem during the fifth and fourth centuries B.C. As G. Ernest Wright and Reginald H. Fuller explain in *The Book of the Acts of God,* it is not only the most widely read book in the Old Testament but may be said to be "a volume of devotional testimony, composed in the light of God's gracious activity. Hymns of praise and thanksgiving, meditations, liturgy for special occasions, the outpouring of souls in a great variety of difficulties—all these are included and many more. While the individual psalms differ greatly in their quality of utterance, even those unlearned in biblical lore cannot fail to be impressed and inspired by the depth of feeling and sheer lyric beauty of many of the psalms, a depth and beauty that appear even in translation. Israel was among the poorest of ancient peoples; yet in literature she surpassed all her contemporaries of western Asia. This is surely not an accident. There was something about the people's faith in God which had an extremely purifying effect both upon the soul and upon the way in which thoughts of the soul were expressed." [9]

As a result, we still depend on the Psalms as an instrument of worship today. They speak to children as well as adults, for the images are vivid and the emotion intense. Our next chapter will include a description of their appeal to a group of children in an inner-city environment, and in the Appendix, psalms especially appropriate for children are listed under "Devotion."

Because the Psalms were useful as a hymnbook in ancient times, it is not surprising that they have inspired musicians and poets through the centuries to set them to music or rephrase them in their own words. This is another reason why psalms are so great a source of enrichment for children. The hymn "Let Us with a Gladsome Mind," for example, is based on Psalm 136, rephrased by John Milton in the seventeenth century. It has been given at least three different musical settings, one of them a Chinese melody. This psalm can be used as motivation for paintings of wonder and thanksgiving, and these, together with choral speaking and the singing of the hymn in whichever musical score is most appropriate, can lift children to new levels of worship. Their involvement will have engaged their minds, their emotions, and their creative acts. A search through church hymnals will reveal other instances of hymn-psalm relationship that can be chosen as an inspiration for painting.

Appreciation of the Bible involves the meaning of moral beauty as well as the poetic and devotional. This we find in many of the stories in the Old Testament, but superbly in accounts of the life of David and the message of the prophets. Every teacher of elementary children should become familiar with the fascinating background and interpretations found in Fleming James' *Personalities of the Old Testament*. Special attention must be called also to the Parables, those matchless stories in the New Testament which Jesus told to convey the truth about God and his kingdom to those who could hear it. An editorial in *The Living Church* recently made this comment about their importance today:

The emphasis upon science has been accompanied by a de-emphasis and neglect of the humanities. Consequently many an "educated" person today is virtually illiterate in the realm of the esthetic and symbolic communication of meaning. Christ's parables speak directly to the heart and will through the imagination, but if so-called "education" serves in practice to suppress and destroy man's imaginative capacity it becomes an obstacle and an enemy to the Gospel. (June 13, 1965.)

This is another reason why painting is of special value to children today and why the Parables provide excellent material for its motivation.

CHAPTER 6

IN ANY KIND OF PARISH

Parishes differ from each other as people do, but children are all alike in needing outlets for their thoughts and feelings whether they live in a city, a suburb, the inner city, or a migrant workers' camp; whether the church is big or little, rich or poor. The degree of need will vary as will the approach to meet it, but this is no novelty among people of Christian concern.

The plight of the migrant workers has been made known to us through the Friendship Press and mission projects attempting to minister to the needs of these people who have no regular church and no home of any kind except the car in which they often sleep and the little temporary cabins near whatever crop they happen to be harvesting. They do not even have an address they can call their own, which means they can neither vote nor get a library card, even if they could read well enough to care. Dr. Robert Coles, a research psychiatrist with the Harvard University Health Services, who has compared hundreds of drawings by both Negro and white children from poor Southern communities, from middle-class suburban areas, and from migrant camps, has reported some of his findings.[1] In the pictures they made of their homes and schools, all the

70

children showed a strong sense of value for both, except the migrant children, who portrayed them carelessly, off to one side as of no account and dwarfed by the trees towering over them. Moreover, they drew them in black crayon and without windows, thus making them, as Dr. Coles explains, a symbol of relationship between a building and the world around. In the past, our literature on service projects has suggested that we send crayons and drawing paper to these children. Painting equipment would be even better to give them a positive experience. In some instances, youth work camps have been organized to offer fellowship and leadership during the summer. These may be only a glimmer of hope, but at least they are a beginning of more active understanding across a most baffling barrier in our midst.

This chapter will undertake to set forth some types of experiences which children have had with painting in different kinds of parishes. In one suburban church in southern New York, new leadership began to transform the church school in less than one year. An unusual painting project in the junior department of this church school is worthy of mention. As the climax to their study of the life of Christ, the children undertook the making of a movie scroll consisting of a series of paintings related to the meaning of Easter. They had learned that the writers of the Gospels had interpreted Jesus' life and mission looking back upon it years later, when they could see the meaning of the whole through the prism of the Resurrection. Accordingly, the first painting was not the betrayal and arrest of Jesus, but the risen Christ revealed to the women at the empty tomb. The second was the Road to Emmaus, and the third, Jesus being beaten at the time of his arrest, followed by the Crucifixion, which was the fourth in order. Because of class discussion on the relationship between the Old and New Testaments, the children included next a picture of the Ten Commandments, which Jesus had come to fulfill. Perhaps the most interesting paintings of all came after the commandments: the first showed two people talking to each other and was intended to suggest the children themselves asking the same crucial question that the followers of Jesus' day had asked: "What does all this mean to us?" In answer, the concluding picture showed a boat with fishermen on board, letting down their nets into the sea. The children wanted to say that the meaning today is the same as in Bible times: to live the way of Jesus as well as to hear it. Coincidentally, this privileged parish began to develop an active relationship with a church in a deprived area, including an exchange of visits and joint meetings for leadership training. This is not to suggest that the exchange was the result of the art project, but that the same meaning was applied in a parallel situation: "Live the Way as well as hear it."

Those who are familiar with work in rural communities where painting has been tried are enthusiastic about the response. Horizons have been lifted and spirits awakened in the church school, and as in other areas, usually under the guidance of the regular volunteer teachers without professional training. One church school superintendent has shared a heartwarming story from his own parish: In the spring, after months of study in relation to a theme of the Bible, teachers received brief instruction in using tempera paint and some principles involved in creative activity as preparation for three successive painting sessions for primary and junior children on Sunday morning. Children were motivated by a review of the major stories they had considered and were given complete freedom to choose the particular event they wished to portray. A boy who had previously been difficult to interest tried an interpretation of the seven lean years from the story of Joseph in Egypt. So well did he catch the feeling of what a farmer would call "seven years of bad luck" that a soil conservationist, acting as a judge of paintings to be sent to an exhibit of children's art, insisted that the boy's picture be included.

A young minister and his wife who have had experience in several rural churches say that their work in creative expression brought quite different results in the three groups where it was tried. In one, they worked with the junior choir in an expanded session which included story and art as well as music. The town itself was unique for that section of the country in that those who held positions of leadership had gone away for higher education and returned with the conviction that they who knew the town well could help it survive and be a responsible community. Farming is dying out there, but these men have done much to attract new industry to this small town, build up the cattle market, bring in cultural and educational advantages. The children in this program, then, came primarily from families who were interested in giving them as many enriching opportunities as possible. With the help of a lay teacher, they were able to build a meaningful short-term project in art as it related to the music they were studying.

The other groups where art was tried were older, including children from the seventh grade up, but they are presented here because they illustrate clearly the place that art can occupy in Christian education. These young people, from farm families scattered about the country, met in "a wonderful rural church out in the middle of someone's cornfield. They were youths deeply involved in the creative forces of life in their simplest form: earth, soil, propagation of crops, the raising of livestock and other animals. Most of them had 4-H involvement; all of them went to school in the county-seat town where a state teachers' college was located. Thus they knew, in a way, the best of two aspects of society, and although they may never leave the farm, they should be infinitely better prepared to lead a fuller life because of their exposure to facts and thoughts outside their primary interest. The results of the experiments with this group were amazing. Form and color, line and abstraction all seemed freeing agents for these youths. Their verbal expression was good; perhaps this helped free them to look for other forms of expression. The results of two experiments stick closely in mind: the Prodigal Son and the parable of the husbandman who entrusted vineyards to tenants who trick him, kill overseers that he sends, and then kill his only son. It was these events and the ensuing consequences that touched some spot of comprehension, some awareness of how much the stories of the Biblical tradition have a relation to our own lives. It was after our work with this painting experience that we were able to move on to Bible study in depth that might never have been reached without art as a means of personal involvement."

The third group was centered in a small, ingrown town where one sixth of the inhabitants were widows, where cousins had intermarried, and the more highly motivated young people had left for better jobs or more education. It was difficult to motivate the group with any kind of program, but in the art project there were one or two thoughtful young people who were willing to open themselves to the new experience. As they did so, however, they were so pressured by the others in the group that they shrank from trying it again. It is probable that the project would have been more successful in a group of elementary-age children less bound by the stagnant thinking of the adult community. In any case, the failure was not due to rural life as such nor to art as a medium, but to the kind of community the residents had permitted to develop.

Turning now to painting as related to the inner city, there are some problems which, although not peculiar to it, do seem more persistent and intense there than in other parishes. Among these is the restlessness of many children, their lack of inner direction, and their difficulty in listening, all of which are related to the tensions and inadequacies of life in the slums. In self-defense against the noise around them, some children turn off their ears, so to speak, and form a habit that is hard to change. They may not hear directions when the teacher gives them. Furthermore, with little cultural help at home, a child's vocabulary may be so meager that he actually does not always understand what the teacher is saying even when he wills to listen. One teacher discovered that several children in her painting group did not know the meaning of the phrase "stroke of the brush." When she demonstrated it, the children were delighted with their new knowledge and promptly made use of it. It may be that painting can help, more than we have realized, to discover a weakness in word power and to overcome it.

Adults who trust themselves and children can do wonders through painting for groups in deprived areas, for as teachers and children come to know each other in a relationship of trust, abilities blossom. Many children of the inner city have a great capacity for appreciation, but they need courage to try new things and reach out to the world as it expands to receive them. Painting with a good friend can help them try.

For those who are willing to undertake such an adventure, it may be helpful to hear how one woman, untrained in art, conducted her first class in such a situation. Holding up a long-handled brush to get attention, she said, "Today you are going to create something all your own, different from anything anyone has ever made before. It will be new and different because you are a person, not exactly like anyone else in the world."

Here and there across an eager face flashed a look of quiet dignity.

"First we will try out our materials," she continued. "Try out anything you wish with your paper and paint. See how it feels to touch your brush to the paper. Try light lines or heavy lines. Try different colors, different shapes, use a wet brush or one almost dry. Don't try to make a picture, just experiment. Use up all your paper. If you need it, you may have a second sheet. O.K. Let's begin."

After fifteen or twenty minutes of delighted activity, the teacher asked the children to lay their experiments on the floor to dry, reassuring them they could paint again in a few minutes. Then everyone moved over to a circle of chairs previously arranged at the other side of the room.

"What makes it possible for us to paint?" asked the teacher, and the answers came tumbling out. "Brushes. Colors. Hands. Eyes. . . ."

"Yes," continued the teacher, "and there's another reason.

We are made in the image of God." She paused for the idea to take hold, then added quickly, "That means we can think and we can imagine. Anything else?"

A little boy raised his hand. "We can love."

"Good. And because God is love, he made a beautiful world for us to live in. I'm going to read you the story about creation in the Bible. Listen carefully, because when I finish, you will have a chance to paint your favorite part of the story."

She opened the Bible and began to read. When she had finished, stopping at the end of the "sixth day," the children returned to the tables. One or two looked puzzled and undecided, and the teacher read the verses again for them. As soon as they "saw" more clearly, they too began to paint. The class had been planned to last an hour, but the children begged to be allowed to stay on for two, and since the teacher was free and the room available, they did.

Neither this account nor the one to follow should be understood as a formula for any other situation. Every teacher must work out her own best way for evoking a response, and it may take trial and error over a period of time to discover it. In fact, the "method" may vary for any teacher with each class, for in addition to planning, creative teaching requires a certain amount of "playing it by ear."

In another church at the other end of the city, this same teacher told a class the story of the Prodigal Son (or, as she called it, the Forgiving Father) to motivate their painting. She stressed the forgiveness freely given by the father to the son, but the painting which followed convinced her that while the children seemed to catch the sequence of events in the parable, they had little real feeling for it. The figure of the father was drawn stiffly, in one case with lifeless arms hanging at his side, a circumstance that seemed to trouble the child afterward as she looked at it. In another picture the paint was badly smeared, and a third child had tried to express forgiveness by painting a cross in each corner as a sign, not an actual part of the picture. One child did express a direct relationship between the meaning of the story and her picture by placing a huge house in the center, indicating her sense of the importance of the son's coming home.

At a second session the same story was tried again, with conversation.

Teacher: How did the father *feel* when he saw his son returning?

Children: He was glad.

Teacher: How do you think he showed it?

A child: Act friendly.

Teacher: Yes, and what did he do?

(No answer.)

At this point Amy, a large and active girl, threw paint on her neighbor's paper deliberately and lost her privilege of painting for a few moments. She objected strenuously, but the teacher was firm.

Teacher (continuing): Let's think about the father again. If he felt friendly, what did he do with his arms?

(No answer.)

Teacher: Did he keep them down at his side or hold them out to his son?

Children: Hold them out.

Teacher: Show me how.

One or two children made a hesitant gesture. The youngest, a child of six, was the most spontaneous. In talking of how the son must have felt when he saw his father coming, the teacher herself knelt down to illustrate an attitude of humility. In this way, through patient, specific questions and a few gestures, the children began to experience the visualization of an image, followed by the attempt to paint it. The paintings on this day were somewhat more relaxed and warmer, the father in several pictures standing with arms outstretched. But the paintings still lacked feeling, were still painted in dull reds and blacks. The teacher was convinced that she had not presented the material with enough feeling herself, or that the children needed more release, or that the story was too complex.

Accordingly, the following week she tried a different approach, which succeeded more than she had had the courage to hope. First, she enthusiastically called the children's attention to the dishes of bright powder paint—red, yellow, blue—then sat with the class in a circle and read portions of the 104th Psalm, which is filled with vivid images: ". . . O Lord my God, thou art very great . . . who hast stretched out the heavens like a tent . . . who makest the clouds thy chariot . . . who ridest on the wings of the wind. . . . Thou makest springs gush forth in the valleys; they flow between the hills. . . . By them the birds of the air have their habitation. . . . The trees of the LORD are watered abundantly. . . . The high mountains are for the wild goats. . . . The sun knows its time for setting. Thou makest darkness, and it is night, when all the beasts of the forest creep forth. . . . Bless the LORD, O my soul! Praise the LORD."

The children listened with keen attention, then each described briefly the image he remembered best. As the last one was given, Amy, who had so troubled the waters the week before, repeated the words softly, "Bless the Lord, O my soul! Praise the Lord." The teacher picked up the cue, and led the entire group in repeating the words together reverently. At the tables a moment later there began a veritable bursting forth in pure color. Something was happening at last, and she saw that it was good.

Still another experience in another parish in the same city will serve to illustrate the wide variety of response to be expected in this kind of work with children from different communities or even from time to time in any given group. When the teacher is unfamiliar with the culture and unacquainted with the children, developments can be especially puzzling. On the day about to be described, ten junior children who lived in Harlem and attended a released-time class clambered eagerly up two flights of stairs to paint in a room at the top of the building—very special because it had two windows open to the light. With only the briefest orientation, the teacher passed out brushes for a tryout period. Joseph began immediately to make an abstract design, but Martin, standing next to him at the table, hesitated to touch the paper with his brush at all. Painting is a kind of commitment, and Martin was not quite ready. Cautiously, he glanced at his confident neighbor, then started to imitate what the other boy was doing. Shortly afterward he spilled paint accidentally on both Joseph's paper and his own, and was so dismayed that the teacher suggested he move to another table where he would have more room, not of course calling attention to the fact that he would also be removed from the temptation to imitate. (Some children could be made conscious of their mistake at this point, but not so insecure a child as Martin appeared to be.) With a fresh sheet of paper, Martin made a fresh start and moved ahead with more assurance. The teacher, although "busy" with her supplies on the other side of the room, kept an eye on what was happening at the tables, and when she saw Martin lay down his brush with a discouraged air, she stepped over to him quietly.

"May I see what you have done?" she asked. Martin uncovered his work, which he had been shielding with his hand. There was the beginning of a boat in strong, firm outline, something she could honestly praise without flattery. "You have made a good beginning," she said, "go ahead and finish it. I hope you will bring it over to show me when it's done."

In another twenty minutes or so Martin was able to show her a sturdy steamboat with flags flying and a fine blue sky overhead. Now it was time for everyone to stop and come into a circle where they listened attentively to the story of Jesus calling Peter and James from their fishing boat to come and follow him. After the story, Martin painted a picture which, together with his comment, indicated far more imagination and perceptiveness than the teacher expected. He had shown a smaller boat this time, with two figures, Peter and James, and, on the green line of the "shore," a third figure, Jesus. Overhead were three birds flying, and a little to one side a spherical green shape. As Martin explained, "Jesus has just called the fishermen. This over here is the green earth, and God, I mean Jesus, is looking at it."

Working with these children brings pleasant surprises. Instead of dashing off immediately after class is finished, they seem to enjoy staying on to help clean up, and know just how to proceed. Many have had wide experience in large families at home and welcome the opportunity to do something for someone else when they know they can do it well. This builds their self-respect and expresses their affection. Another surprise is the refreshing honesty of the children, who apparently have little use for pretense. "You're wearing a new coat today," said one girl to her teacher. "It don't look so good on you." Finally, there is the bubbling enthusiasm with which a special enterprise is undertaken. Most children enjoy sharing their creative work, but to those of the inner city there is deep significance in being able to "point with pride," both among themselves and those of other races. When painting is a continuing activity, an exhibit is indispensable as a crowning joy.

To give children of any parish a continuing experience of painting will require persistent concern and additional people. Neighboring parishes may want to pool their resources for a mutually rewarding association. Volunteers from at least one suburban church near New York have been going once a week to teach in a critical area after school, and in some parishes individuals have begun to "adopt" children culturally. A trip to an art museum for a small group or for just one child who knows little of adult companionship can be significant. A child of the slums needs to know that the big world outside is not inaccessible, that it is even accessible to him. Through being introduced to new experiences in his own neighborhood and beyond, he can learn that his world is not so narrow after all, that he can reach out and become something better than he used to think possible. The Church has a genius for caring whenever the members exercise it, and opportunities for imaginative ways to help children are waiting to be discovered by those who can lose their fear of the untried. God in Christ made himself completely available by letting himself be com-

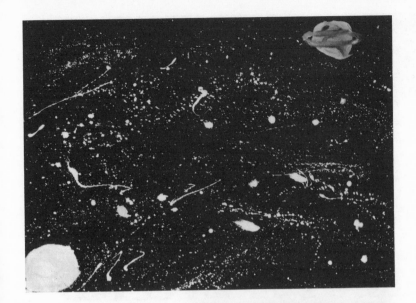

"This is the Universe in which everything is." By an eleven-year-old girl.

"This is Abraham praying." One of a series of windows in a fourth-grade group project.

"The disciples are getting the colt." By a nine-year-old boy.

"The main yellow is the angel and the yellow extending down to the figure is the glory that Mary feels." The Annunciation by a ten-year-old boy.

"I try to show his light is still there." The Empty Tomb by an eleven-year-old girl.

"This is a spring picture. I have made the roses especially big." The Resurrection by a ten-year-old girl.

"God helping my grandpa that died . . . in a rainbow and snow."
By a five-year-old girl.

Japanese fishing scene by an eight-year-old boy.

pletely vulnerable. This is the kind of love which can cast out fear in the context of our daily lives wherever we may be called to live them. "Clothe yourselves, all of you, with humility toward one another . . . under the mighty hand of God . . . Cast all your anxieties on him, for he cares about you." (1 Peter 5:7 RSV.)

In Summary

Painting is a way for children to express their joy and is in itself a means of joy.

Painting is a way to release tension.

Painting helps a child to know acceptance.

Painting helps a child to understand himself and others, the world about him, and God.

Painting helps a child to grow in confidence and initiative.

Painting helps a teacher understand a child and guide him in Christian nurture.

Painting is a way to clarify religious concepts and strengthen their meaning.

Painting is a way to give a child an experience of fellowship.

Painting is a way to give a child an experience of commitment.

Painting is a way to enrich a child's life through appreciation of the work of others, including the great masters of religious art.

Painting is a way to develop in a child an awareness of beauty.

Painting helps to lay a foundation for spiritual and aesthetic enrichment in maturity.

For no other subject is capable of giving the child consciousness in which image and concept, sensation and thought, are correlated and unified. . . .

Herbert Read [2]

That art has a fundamental influence on the child's personality growth, and therefore on his future, is a fact which has been determined beyond any doubt.

Viktor Lowenfeld [3]

PART II

Practical Helps
for the Teacher

CHAPTER 7

PROCEDURES

When to Paint

Paint as often as possible! In the past many churches have been content to wait until the summer vacation school to provide painting, but there are at least two ways to have painting all year. One is to establish weekday periods for after-school activities at the church in which art is one of the choices. In this way a full hour can be made available, and only those who are truly interested come, so that the teaching conditions can be excellent. The disadvantage of this plan is that the objective of reaching as many children as possible is not achieved. To do this, and to relate the art closely to the Sunday class, there is no reason why an entire Sunday morning cannot occasionally be given to painting—either as one of the ways to develop a unit, at the end of a unit, or for some other special reason—and certainly without a sense of guilt!

In some communities Saturday morning is a convenient time for an activity period. Children at one church in a Chicago suburb do not come every week, but they have participated in a successful experiment that included painting on the Saturday mornings of Advent and on the Family Nights during

Lent. Families can paint together for fellowship as described in Chapter 4. Here again, each parish must work out its own salvation in creative art.

Who Should Paint?

If the session is held on Sunday morning, and space is adequate, the entire class should be involved as a matter of course. (If a child for some unknown reason objects to joining in, the situation would have to be explored, of course.) If the room is crowded, groups can take turns during the morning if time permits, using both tables and floor, or one of the groups can wait until the following week. Team teaching makes this kind of arrangement possible. If the painting is to be a weekday activity, the number should be limited to ten unless there is to be a co-teacher or assistant. The interest of the children and their behavior can be a determining factor for attendance during the week, especially if the teacher is inexperienced. She will serve the children best if she does not undertake too much at first.

The painting will be more interesting if both boys and girls are in the same group, but there should be not more than a two- or three-year age span unless it is a special family session, which naturally would contain a wide range of ages. In the context of painting, the educational process can be promoted best over a period of time in a group of approximately the same level of development. For example, to have adolescents painting next to primary children, still in the symbolic stage, can be confusing to both.

Where to Paint

A light, airy room with windows is ideal. If there is distracting traffic outside, the curtains or blinds should be closed, but if there is a pleasant view, it can be an inspiration in itself. It must be reiterated, however, that children working in basements without windows and with only feeble electric bulbs overhead have made pictures of meaning and beauty.

Young children enjoy painting on the floor, while the older primaries and juniors prefer standing at a table. Easels are not necessary, and chairs are in the way. There must be plenty of space for materials and for free arm movement. If the tables are too narrow for the size of the paper, the children should work at one side only. If the room is large, and individual tables are available, they can be arranged in a circle or a hollow square. This helps to create a climate of relatedness in spite of the intensely individual nature of painting. The teacher's "desk" can be one of the tables in the circle, and if plenty of space is left between tables, she can move freely about, or see all the children's faces without moving at all. The room is also likely to be more quiet when children are not crowded in with their backs to each other.

Setting Up the Room

First, one should think through what has to be done, and allow more time to do it than seems necessary. Both time and trouble will be saved if a room can have its own built-in storage space for all the necessary supplies, as well as shelves and drawers wide enough to store large paper and the finished paintings until time to share them in some way or take them home. One church built a new cupboard which fitted neatly into a corner between two doors and included not only the usual shelves for paper of varied sizes, but also vertical slots for oak tag, poster board, and mats for mounting pictures. There was also space below for bulky supplies. Each of the cupboard doors was realistically fitted with a lock and key.

A sink is important for water supply and washing up, and a whole row of sinks would be too good to be true! Custodians do not seem to appreciate it when children wash paint dishes in the general lavatories of the building. Somewhere near the sink there should be a supply of paper towels, soap, a can of cleanser, and a large sponge.

Materials

Tables should be protected by newspapers, and all materials laid out, before the children arrive so the teacher will be free to greet them as they come in. Preparing ahead also saves precious time for the purpose in hand. This means that a large sheet of paper, a long-handled brush, a small piece of sponge, a plastic bowl or coffee can filled with water (for rinsing the brush or sponge), and a paper towel will be ready at each place in addition to the paint: red, yellow, and blue (the three primary colors), plus black, white, and possibly brown. If a class continues, other colors such as purple or aqua blue may be added. If the brush is laid across the paper it lends an air of readiness when the children come in, an invitation to create. For children who may not be self-disciplined, however, it is better to pass out the brushes only after the orientation is completed.

Dry tempera powder is simpler to use than wet paint, for it is less expensive, easier to prepare, and easier to store. The powder can be poured directly from the spout into individual containers to be used by each child or shared two and two if necessary. These containers may be sections of egg-cup trays, which any grocer who buys eggs by the crate will be glad to give away. The trays can be cut up into sections of six, arranged in three pairs each. At the end of the session they can be stacked with a Kleenex or shirt board between each layer for safekeeping.

If wet paint is preferred, it can be bought ready-mixed or in powder form at half the price and mixed by the leader. Whichever way is chosen, wet paint takes longer to prepare. A separate spatula for each color is necessary to stir the paint with before using it, and a separate dessert spoon for each color is necessary to ladle it from the jars to the paint pots. Unless the pots are stackable, they will have to be washed afterward. One could use five or six glass furniture coasters set on an aluminum tray for each child. This arrangement is pleasant to use, because the tray holds his other supplies in neat array and also serves as a palette for mixing colors, but it does represent an expenditure of money as well as time to keep the trays and coasters clean even when they can be stacked. Even if the budget is adequate, many volunteer teachers could not give the time required. (Since these are the people who will have to be depended on in most church schools, how much time they are asked to spend must be within reason.) But to return to tools: a tin pot-lid can be used as a palette, or one of the less glossy TV dinner containers. (The shiny ones are too slippery.) In the past, teachers have used muffin tins to hold wet paints, but the disadvantage is that the leftover colors cannot be poured back into the jars. Muffin tins could be used for the dry powder if satisfactory egg cartons are not available. Other inventive ideas for paint dishes include the small, deep, metal tops of instant-coffee jars, individual ice-cube cups, or even small paper drinking cups (which are, however, both awkward and perishable).

Although children can always share their materials with their neighbors, it is a great help if they do not have to. Painting can be difficult unless well organized. Accidents happen more easily when supplies are passed around or dipped into indiscriminately, and children more readily learn responsibility for their own equipment and respect for that of others when there is enough for all and boundaries are definite. It should also be understood that only the leader in charge has access to the large cans of powder or the jars of paint. Only in this way can she be sure that the red spoon does not get into the blue jar, and so on, until no pure color is left.

The First Session

Begin with as few words as possible. The purpose is not to talk about painting, but to paint. If it is the very first time the children have met to paint with this teacher, however, they should gather for a brief orientation in chairs previously arranged away from the working area. The teacher may want to help them become aware of the dignity of painting, possibly in some such way as the visiting teacher did with the children in Harlem, as described in Chapter 6. God is the Creator and never stops creating. We are made in his image, and when we use our ability to think and feel and imagine, we share with him a little of the great venture of creation. If the teacher feels this deeply, the children, too, will understand it. Then, in a climate of expectancy, she can explain the few simple procedures. If she does not have a sincere conviction about this part of the orientation, she should begin in some other way that she prefers, or possibly just with the few necessary directions such as the following points, expressed in her own words:

Each child should have all the supplies he needs, but they must not be wasted.

Materials must be respected and cared for.

A brush too full of water can be stroked on the side of the dish (if the word *stroke* is not understood, the teacher may demonstrate what she means with a brush and paint dish).

If dry powder is used, the brush is dipped first in water, then in the powder, and finally applied to the paper either pure or mixed. If a second pure color is desired, the brush must be rinsed between colors.

Volunteers from the class should be enlisted in advance to help clean up. It is wise to limit the number to two or three.

The first day will be a day of discovery, of trying out the materials and experimenting for fun.

Beginners can see how it feels to make contact with their brush on paper, or how many kinds of lines and shapes they can make and which colors they find most pleasing.

If the large sheet is filled quickly, a second can be used if desired.

Those who have painted before can experiment with brush strokes new to them, or with mixing tints and shades by adding more or less water.

At this point the teacher will ask the children to go to the tables quietly and begin. If the group is a large one and she has an assistant, she can divide the children into two groups to avoid confusion. It is best to begin in an orderly way, which may even seem pedantic, until the teacher knows what to expect; later she can be as informal as circumstances will permit. As the period progresses, she may see some children proceeding with confidence, others timidly, using only part of their space; she can offer quiet praise or encouragement if it is needed. For the most part, however, few suggestions should be given so that the interests and abilities of the children, as well as their needs, can be expressed without self-consciousness or interference. There should be no comparing and evaluating competitively, but each child's painting should be appreciated for its own sake. Just as it is, it is of value because it is his own personal expression. Later, if the group continues, the children will feel free to talk with each other about their paintings honestly and with mutual appreciation.

When a child completes his painting, the teacher should ask him what he would like to tell her about it, and should take down the comment word for word (on the back of the painting if it is dry, otherwise on a slip of paper with his name, age, grade, and the date, to be pasted or taped on the back later for future reference). If there is no comment, the child should not be prodded into making any. It is spontaneous verbalizing, not forced, which is helpful to the child in self-knowledge, and to parent or teacher as an indication of the child's understanding of religious truth. If a child should say, in a tone of awe, "I can't express it," it is possible he has had a very rich experience indeed. On the other hand, if the answer is an uncommunicative "uh-uh," whatever the experience has been, that is all he intends to say about it and his silence should be respected. As rapport and confidence develop, even a nonverbal child may be encouraged to talk about his work.

The comment is a most important step in the painting experience because it is not only a self-evaluation of the work but a clarification to himself and the teacher of what he is thinking, feeling, and believing. It completes the creative act for him and rounds out his communication for others. If the entire first session is given over to experimentation, neither the comment nor any other form of evaluation is likely to have the same degree of interest which subsequent sessions will produce when there is motivation by specific subject matter. Still, if there is time, it is a good idea to have a show-and-tell period to give the children an opportunity to share their discoveries with each other and take a step in getting acquainted. The tone of this period should be friendly, not critical, marked by mutual respect instead of competition.

If a great deal of paint has been used on any of the paintings, they will have to be left to dry on the table or the floor or in some other prearranged place where they will not be disturbed. It is wise to ask that all paintings be left in the church for the time being until plans for sharing them with others have been made. When the day's work is dry, the leader-in-charge should see that it is stored away safely or put up for display.

The Second Session

The procedure for a second session will be similar to the first except that there will be a presentation of the subject matter instead of an orientation. This is sometimes called the "motivation," that significant moment of being "moved." Through the reading or telling of a Bible story or some other relevant material, the imagination is kindled, the feelings stirred, the mind stimulated to create.

For beginning teachers the following suggestions may help in preparing their children in advance for alert and imaginative listening:

1. Ask the children to watch for certain things as the story is presented, such as: What time of day is it? What is happening? If you were there, what would you see? what would you hear? how would you feel? Try to imagine how the people in the story are feeling. (These reminders can also be written on the board.)

2. Introduce the story briefly.

3. Present the story clearly, vividly, with feeling.

4. Without further discussion, let the children paint.

From here on the second session will be much like the first except that response to well-prepared subject matter may be more concentrated and intense than in a tryout period. Although the subject is the same for all, pictures will be different except in the case of an insecure child who may imitate his neighbor in the beginning.

If painting is planned as an integral part of the Sunday-morning program, there is no problem of special preparation of the subject matter. It will already have taken place in the natural course of the unit of study. If it is scheduled as a week-day activity, and led by the regular teacher, there is still no problem. If the painting group is conducted by someone unrelated to the Sunday class, and the members come because of special interest rather than class enrollment, so that they have been variously prepared, then it is important that a coordinator check with the teachers and offer to the weekday leader any suggestions for material that might be relevant and helpful, possibly a "fact sheet." Chapter 9 includes examples of brief introductions to Bible stories which can be prepared as guidelines by either the coordinator or one of the other teachers involved. The weekday teacher will be able to work with her group most creatively, however, if she supplements these guidelines with her own personal preparation, even to the point of "struggle." If the story comes alive for her, it will reach the children. The story presentation should keep to the Bible account in event and spirit, rather than any individual interpretation of it, even when it must be retold or elaborated for some groups to understand. It is often surprising how much even Biblically illiterate children catch from the Bible itself if the reading is well done. Mrs. Marcus Barth, in a talk to a group of Christian educators, said that when telling Bible stories to deprived children in Chicago she never watered them down but let the Bible make its own sharp impact. Each teacher will have to find her own way in this as in other procedures. One thing is sure, no matter how dramatic the story is itself, a dull presentation will evoke only dull painting.

Summary of Proposed Sessions

First Session	*Second Session*
Greetings	Greetings
Orientation, with the group seated away from the working area	Presentation of subject to children at tables
Tryout time to discover materials	The painting
Comment of child written down as pictures dry	Comment of child written down
Show-and-tell if time permits	Show-and-tell (now or next week)
Clean-up time with help of parents or children; or both	Clean-up time
Paintings posted or safely stored	Paintings posted or safely stored

Note: If painting is to be continuing activity, a tryout period should be provided every so often, either for an entire session or for fifteen or twenty minutes at the beginning.

Never wash a brush in hot
water (loosens bristles)
Always dry brushes in
open coffee can or pitcher

Children like to experiment
with mixing colors, but the
child who needs reassurance
may be helped by a simple
chart like the one below.

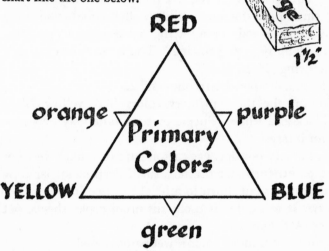

RED

orange — purple
Primary
Colors
YELLOW ———— BLUE
green

Red + Blue = Purple
Blue + Yellow = Green   } Secondary
Red + Yellow = Orange   Colors

Check List of Supplies

Tables: 1 small table for each child is ideal. Children working at large tables must have room for arm movements and for large sheets of paper.

Paper: Size 18 x 24 inches.

Manila preferred, newsprint or wrapping paper. Regular newspapers can be used if necessary; the print may show through, but will not spoil the fun.

Brushes: 1 for each child. Long-handled (10 to 12 inches). Flat (½ or ¾ inches wide) with fairly stiff bristles. The round or pointed brush of soft camel's hair is less desirable for children since it does not make contact with the paper as well. Several smaller brushes, however, should be available for children if they request them for details.

Sponge: 1 small piece for each child. (A household sponge cut in quarters.) Good for applying a wash, or using large strokes, dabbing, or "printing." The corners can be used for "drawing" lines.

Paint: Tempera, dry powder recommended.

Minimum: the three primary colors (red, yellow, blue) plus black and white. (Purple or aqua blue may be added later for interest.)

Paint cups: For dry powder: egg-carton cups or muffin tins. For mixed paint: furniture coasters, small deep metal jar tops, or milk cartons cut down to a height of two inches.

Mixing trays: If wet paint is used: rustproof cooky sheets, pot lids, or TV-dinner trays.

Dessert spoons: To transfer color if wet paint is used.

Newspapers: To protect tables.

Paper towels: To try out brush or remove excess moisture.

Coffee cans: 1 for each child to hold water for rinsing brush.
1 for each table for stacking brushes, bristles up!

Smock: 1 man's shirt for each child with sleeves cut short or rolled.

Buckets: To carry water in if the room has no sink.

CHAPTER 8

GUIDANCE

As in all guidance, guiding children through art is less a matter of rule than of relationship. It is a dialogue at a deep level between the children and their teacher, and among the children themselves. When God is present, the spirit is Holy, which explains the good that flowers in and through joy, acceptance, growth, understanding, and fellowship. It is the Good Shepherd guiding his flock, leaving neither the children nor the teacher to struggle alone.

Is Training Necessary?

Although the quality of spirit is of first importance to teachers and children, they also need the assurance that comes from a practical knowledge of their undertaking, a fact which leads one to ask how much training the leader of a painting group needs. In the context of Christian education, this question should be preceded by three others: Does the prospective teacher like children and have a concern for their best possible development? Is she convinced that painting is a valuable instrument for this purpose? Is she open to experimentation and learning through experience? If an adult can answer these questions affirmatively, he or she is ready without professional training to learn a few simple procedures that will enable her to conduct a painting session with satisfactory and perhaps rewarding results. If she cannot, she will not be desirable as a teacher in our frame of reference, even though highly trained. Many children will have had previous art experience in day school as a foundation, and a workshop in advance can prepare untrained teachers to make a beginning, especially if the project is to be a short one, or if the painting is to be done in connection with a unit of material in the church school. In the Oregon project already referred to, parent volunteers were urged to remove themselves from the working area after getting the children started, and to offer no suggestions or help unless obviously necessary in some routine connection.

If a church wishes to continue the painting sessions throughout the school year, or during the summer, it will be important for the teacher to add to her knowledge and experience in order to understand the developing needs of the children and to give simple guidance either to those who have had little previous experience in painting or to those who need to widen their horizons. She will bear in mind the basic principle that her role is not to teach technique but to help the child express his own ideas in his own way. It is better to give no guidance than to give too much, for it is the enjoyment and the practice of art in general that provides the best teaching at the younger age-levels. Following the workshop, the nonspecialist teacher will learn through experience in a teaching situation, by reading, by observation, even by getting the "feel" of it herself by painting at home. Her purpose is not to push for an end product in a vocational sense, not to teach *art* (which should be done by a professional), but to teach children *through* art to understand themselves and their faith. She will become interested in an art skill if it will help a child express a more sensitive idea and a deeper feeling, or to express them more beautifully, especially if the child is honestly reaching for these and asking for help, or requires it as a stimulus to come out of a groove.

Introductory Workshop for Teachers

In a teacher's workshop the room should be set up as it would be for a children's class so that prospective leaders can see how supplies and equipment are handled. It should be pointed out, however, that each teacher will have to adapt her own arrangement to the space and furnishing of the church. Conditions may be nearly ideal, or they may require the utmost ingenuity. If the group is to be a small one, and individual tables are available, they can be placed in a circle or a square for fellowship as described in the previous chapter. An easy-to-listen-to recording of a symphony orchestra, played as the teachers come in, can lift the spirits whether the workshop takes place after a long day or on a Saturday morning. Just as for the children, the materials should be ready at each place, offering an invitation to paint.

There are two ways to begin, either immediately at the tables, standing for the orientation, or taking chairs first in another part of the room and moving to the tables after the orientation. The content and manner of this opening, which should be kept brief, will depend on the leader's preference and the interests of the class members. A leader may want to follow a statement about the gift of creativity with a prayer of thanksgiving before introducing the materials. If there is a prayer, it should not be formal or thought of in terms of a "devotional," which tends to become perfunctory and too long, but a simple lifting up of mind and heart in gratitude for whatever the leader is moved to be thankful for, whether it is natural beauty, or the beauty of holiness, or the joy of creative expression. The prayer should also be brief. The purpose of the workshop is painting, not worship, although the painting will be more meaningful if it is done in a worshipful spirit, which may or may not require "visible" prayer.

The leader should introduce the tools of painting in such a way that anyone without knowledge of the simplest procedures can learn enough to be able to conduct a session with children herself. She will show the class the supplies they are to use, holding up each one in turn with a brief explanation: "We use a long-handled brush for greater freedom of the arm, a sponge for variety in painting effects, a coffee can or plastic bowl for water to rinse brush or sponge, a paper towel to absorb water from a brush too full of water," and so on. This part of the orientation may have to be more detailed for the teachers than the children, who are likely to be familiar with painting equipment. If they are not, the teachers can duplicate the experience they are having at the workshop. The chapter on procedures can be reread for suggestions. It will be especially important to insist the workers do not try consciously to make a picture but just "let go" and see what it is like to paint freely any kind of line or shape or color. It is not possible for adults to step back entirely into the kind of free expression they may have known as children, but they can try. One thing is certain, they will have fun. Before laying the experiments aside to dry on empty tables or the floor, the class will enjoy seeing each other's work in a short show-and-tell exchange at the tables. The leader has a special function to set everyone at ease in the same spirit of acceptance that each will try to provide in her own class when the time comes. She can also draw out from the teachers what they have learned so far. What have they noticed about mixing colors? Did they find out for the first time how to mix green? Or purple? Or had they mixed colors before? Any other discoveries? She can ask if someone would like to explain the primary colors, and why they are called by that name. The leader will want to supply whatever information is missing. Possibly no one knows that in this case *primary* means "basic," and that from the three (red, yellow, blue) all other colors can be made; or that black will darken a color and white will lighten it. This would be a good time to show the simple chart on page 99, which they can use with children. More elaborate charts are not recommended, because it is more creative for children to discover the harmonies that please them best, leaving the textbook rules until later, perhaps until junior high. The value of the simple chart will be discussed later in the chapter.

For the motivation, members of the workshop will move to the area where chairs have been set up. The leader will have prepared her material carefully, preferably something which the teachers can use with their own classes: a psalm with vivid imagery and strong feeling, perhaps, or a story from the Old Testament with plenty of action, or the story of the Creation, or something from the New Testament, such as one of the Parables or an event from the life of Jesus. The leader should explain that if painting is done on Sunday morning, study of the subject matter will already have taken place in the natural course of events, so that on the day when painting is done, the only motivation will be the direct reading of the story or perhaps just a quick review of the events. If the class is scheduled during the week and taught by someone other than the Sunday teacher, there should be a brief background presentation before the story is read. Some leaders prefer to read the story to the group as they stand ready at the tables so that painting may begin whenever an inspiration occurs. The choice of method may depend on the age of those attending the training session. Older people may prefer to sit for the story as well as for the painting, whereas both children and younger teachers usually like to stand for better control of the material and greater freedom of arm movement. As each painting is finished, the leader will proceed just as she will advise the teachers to do with their children, taking down the comment (if any) to be pasted on the back of the painting when it is dry. If the workshop is a large one, the leader will need help for this.

Although the comment is part of the evaluation, there should be a show-and-tell experience before the group breaks up. Each person takes her painting to the chair area and holds it up for all to see. The leader can ask each to tell about her work in the order in which people are seated, or here and there as eagerness may indicate. If an informal atmosphere has prevailed during the session, this period will be one of real enjoyment. Members will feel free not only to talk about their own work, but to express appreciation of that of others and to ask questions. The teacher will contribute now and then if it seems appropriate, but she should not monopolize the sharing period. As with children, she should avoid a critical attitude in terms of any conventional art standards of evaluation. Praise for a pleasing combination of colors, an unusual arrangement of objects, or for making an idea clear is better than pointing out how perspective or proportion has been violated. If such matters are brought up by someone in the group, the leader should explain the principle she recommends regarding technique for elementary children. (It will seldom be appropriate for adults.)

If the workshop is not to be followed by a second the following week, the teachers will want to take their paintings home. If they are to return, the leader can post the paintings in the meantime so the teachers will have experienced the complete sequence they will be giving the children.

A large group of forty or fifty teachers could be conducted in the same way as the small group except that the painting should be done in a larger room and probably at long dining-room tables arranged not in a circle, but so as to catch the light from the windows or light fixtures overhead. For a group of this size, a leader would need several assistants to help arrange supplies, to carry water if none is available in the room, and to help clean up afterward. This is a task of no small proportions, but each trainee can help by washing her own brush and sponge, throwing her own paper towels in the basket, folding up the newspapers which have been protecting the tables. It is also helpful to use dry paint instead of wet to avoid the tedious work of washing jars and paint pots. If the workshop can be conducted by a team of three co-teachers, careful planning will make it possible to give more help to each table as the work proceeds. It would be ideal if, following this initial workshop, the group could observe a demonstration lesson with children, or help to plan and teach in a laboratory class followed by evaluation. Whenever possible, an opportunity for in-service training should also be provided later in the year.

Indirect and Direct Guidance

Everything in this book is related to guidance in one form or another—indirectly through the releasing power of creative love, directly through the animating resources of the Christian faith. To guide is not to dictate or dominate, but to draw forth the potential power within to help make the person whole. It is also to inform, to give specific knowledge in a specific situation. The former we may call indirect guidance, the latter direct.

Several ways of providing indirect guidance in the field of art have already been described in Part I. Two further illustrations on the use of conversation for this purpose are given below. They are taken from personal experience.

A boy of nine who was painting an animal for a group mural suddenly scribbled over it and the teacher came to his side to ask casually: "Having trouble?" "It's no good," replied the child in discouragement.

"What is it you don't like?"

"I can't remember how a wolf's head goes."

"Is it round or pointed?"

"Pointed."

"Are the ears big and floppy?"

"No, they're pointed."

"O.K. You have made a good body. Go ahead and try again."

In a few moments the boy had made a fine new wolf and was enthusiastically beginning on a cage for it to sleep in.

Another boy had just finished painting a dog and brought his picture to show the teacher, asking, "Do you think this is a good dog?"

She guessed that he was not satisfied with his work and was asking for help more than encouragement.

"The back of your dog is splendid, and so is his tail, but the head. . . . What do *you* think of the head?" (It was unrecognizable.)

"I don't think it's so good."

"Do you have a dog at home?"

"No, but there's one on our street."

"Well," advised the teacher, "take a good look at his head the next time you see him, and then draw what you remember as soon as possible."

This is a more creative approach than taking the child's pencil and drawing a dog for him to copy, even if that is what he asks. When we encourage or permit a child to copy, we deny him real thought, imagination, initiative, and independence. We hinder his growth as a person.

Conversation can also disclose other reasons for inexpressive work. Perhaps the environment is not stimulating, in which case steps must be taken to provide perceptual experiences such as those described in the chapter on appreciation. Or one may discover that a child is unable to hear directions because he does not understand the teacher's vocabulary. If a city child has never seen a path, he will not understand the phrase "paths of righteousness," even though he is old enough to think symbolically. Guidance involves not only providing information but searching out the range of word-power by which knowledge can be communicated. The Commonwealth School in Boston, first independent school to open its doors to a 10 per cent Negro enrollment, has been working sacrificially with those children whose limited vocabulary prevents their native intelligence from coping with advanced ideas. In religious education through art, we too can pioneer in closing the vocabulary gap as well as bridging the concept chasm.

From previous chapters it will be clear that direct guidance is not as highly recommended for elementary children as indirect. There are always exceptions, and there are times when one merges into the other. Then only experience can show what is best in any given situation. If a child asks, "How do you make green?" the sensible answer is "Mix yellow with blue." If the same child continues to ask the same or similar questions over a period of time and shows no initiative, he should be asked to experiment and discover for himself, or be referred to a simple color chart.

Tryout-Period Experiments

The tryout period is a good time to experiment with short tasks or problems that will help provide ease in handling materials in an interesting way without pushing the children beyond their level of development. The following suggestions can help develop perceptual awareness as well as skill.

1. Paint a portrait of yourself or a member of your family. Is the face round or long? What color are the eyes and hair? Try to paint as you remember (feel your face but don't look in the mirror), but bear in mind you are not a photographer and can leave out some things, or add a few. This is the fun of being an artist!

2. Paint a portrait of an angel, a shepherd, Mary, or Jesus.

3. Make a wash over the paper, then paint "into it" with a darker tone. A sponge is good for this.

4. Mix one color with another; mix various colors together to see how they neutralize each other.

5. Take one color and see how many tints you can make of it.

6. Notice how each color looks in relation to the paper and how it changes as more color is added.

7. Try opaque white, then a wash of white, over various colors already dry. This gives a misty effect, and variety in texture.

8. Try an "overlay" of color. Paint a light or dark background with brush strokes, letting it dry before painting other colors or washes on top.

9. Spatter paint from a full brush on either a wet or dry wash.

10. Try to make a crowd of people: round faces looking toward the viewer; people with their backs to the viewer; people sideways in a procession. (These may be made by single vertical strokes in different colors if desired.)

11. Experiment with making trees: Try letting the white paper show through green masses to look like light shining through.

12. Try to make a sky that looks sunny or one that looks stormy.

13. Try painting with your sponge.

14. Try making lines with the handle of your brush.

15. Try painting your feelings: love, hate, fear, excitement, wonder, peace. (Best when motivated, as below.)

16. Recall a strong feeling for a person or place and try to paint it: A circus? storm? party? forest? mountain? sea?

17. You say you don't know how to paint rain? Try an eraser to make slanting lines across the picture. Or the handle of your brush. Or white paint. Experiment!

Untrained teachers may find the following hints helpful even though they will never use them unless a child asks or obviously needs help. To clutter up the minds of children with unnecessary information before they start to paint, no matter how interesting it may be to the teacher, will only confuse them. They may already know all they need to know.

On using a brush:

Hold it like a pencil, relaxed yet firm, high or low on the handle as suits you best.

Use a horizontal hold when adding colors over an area already painted.

You can stroke the paint on, dab it on, or drip it on.

The brush can be almost dry (which makes an interesting texture), or quite full, as you require.

On color:

To get intense color, use it pure with very little water.

Notice that a wet color is darker than a dry one.

On organizing the paper:

Keep it simple. Make it big: big paper, big strokes. If a child feels more secure using small paper and small strokes, he should be given this privilege.

Warning!

DON'T *say these things:*

1. "Stroke your brush with assurance. Don't be so jerky."
Calling attention to tension only increases it. Help a child to
FEEL assured and his painting will become so.

2. "Have a center of interest in your picture." If a child
is strongly motivated, he will HAVE an interest and know where
to put it in the way that is right for him.

3. "Make decisions before you start." By "decisions" here
we refer to the child's making his mind up about such questions as: Do I want a vertical picture or a horizontal one?
Where shall I put my horizon?
These matters are best dealt with unconsciously by younger
children and by older children, if necessary, in a show-and-tell
period. To insist on preliminary pondering can blunt a creative
edge.

*4. "If you want to show grandeur, make your sky three-
quarters of the picture."* Children should be helped to FEEL
grandeur, not learn a rule. Moreover, a picture that is three-
quarters mountain is also grand.

5. "Don't use too many details." Most children do not
need this advice, so why bother them? If a child habitually tries
to handle more than he can, however, he might find such advice
reassuring.

Some Useful Pointers

On Perspective:

If a child is really eager to know something about perspective and figure drawing, there are several ways a nonprofessional
teacher can satisfy his interest. He can tell him a few principles
and make a few suggestions:

1. Perspective is a matter of representing three dimen-
sions on a two-dimensional surface. This involves proportion
and distance between objects.

2. The usual way to show a distant object is to put it higher on the paper than the near one, and to paint it smaller and more dimly, with less vivid colors, less sharp outline.

3. The close object is larger, clearer, sharper.

4. The child can start observing how the lines go on a door or a chair and try to draw these the way they look to him.

5. Railroad tracks and roads look wider apart close by; they seem to meet in the far distance.

6. Some painters ignore these rules: Grandma Moses, for example, and Henri Rousseau and some Oriental artists.

On Figure Drawing:

1. Some teachers like to give rules about what proportion of the body is taken up by the head, the torso, the legs, and so on. For our purposes, it is best to ask the child to observe people in real life and then try to draw them: people at home, standing or sitting; people on the street running, buying a newspaper, or waving to a taxi.

2. It is helpful to suggest noticing where the body bends: at the neck, the elbow, the hips, and so forth.

3. The child can be reminded that not all details need to be included. Some can be left out, some merely suggested.

4. Children can draw simple figures to suit their own age and interests without being taught, and untrained teachers are not equipped to lead children over twelve, or those unusually gifted, in technical figure drawing.

CHAPTER 9

SUBJECT MATTER

Subject matter for painting in Christian education has been discussed incidentally throughout the preceding chapters, but further guidelines may be helpful. Choice of subject matter is based on whether it is suitable for the age of the children, whether it will interest them, and whether it is relevant to the Christian faith. Each of these criteria is a check against the other. Stories of horror and violence must interest children or they would not be produced commercially, yet they fail the test of suitability. Action and suspense can get attention, but unless they involve an idea worthy of a human child, they will produce a morbid rather than a creative stimulus. Again, a story with a good idea may be expressed in adult terms which are inappropriate. Some Bible stories have to be retold in simpler words for primary children, and for juniors some have to be condensed to essentials without being watered down so that the point of the story is lost. So much research has been done by the major denominations that a beginning teacher can be guided by the curriculum as to what is suitable for the different age-groups. For those who like to explore the field and rethink each unit afresh, further treasures can be discovered.

Well-chosen subject matter will do more to give children

enjoyment and control of their art materials than exercises of technique. Even if we were to teach a class art as such (rather than art as an integral part of Christian education), the Judaeo-Christian heritage would still be an excellent resource because it meets the criteria for good motivation: it is dramatic, evokes deep personal feeling, and deals with themes of universal value. Neither art nor religion is born of trivial thought or feeling. In a world overshadowed by mass production and easy speed, those aspects of the human story which tell of personal struggle, growth, and faith, stand out as an uncommon instrument for educating children.

According to Susanne Langer, symbol and meaning contribute to man's world far more than does sensation. This is one reason why children should be provided with something more than perfunctory ideas and experiences. There is nothing wrong with a trip to the grocery store as a subject for art, but it simply does not challenge the best in a child unless it is lifted in some way above the mundane. Common things become uncommon when seen with eyes of appreciation, an insight with which Marion Richardson revolutionized the teaching of art in English schools, but somewhere along the way there must be transcendent material to inspire that kind of vision. Paul Tillich has said that although man has a natural inclination toward meaning and reality, it can be awakened "only through a content which comes into the field of vision of the child, in his daily life and in special hours of consecration. The child must be grasped by this content even if he does not understand it intellectually, and the content must transcend the child in awe and meaning so that he is always attracted in longing and awe. Such are religious symbols, wherever they are alive and understood. They unite a definite form with an infinite meaning which evokes creativity." [1] Daily bread, for example, becomes more than a morsel of food through the Lord's Prayer and the Lord's Supper. The spirit of Christ expressed in words and action transforms the meaning for us.

For obvious reasons, the inherited material of our faith is

the backbone of the teaching in our church schools. Many children are not likely to encounter it anywhere else. As for Christian parents, they come to feel when they enter the strange world of the Bible that in spite of its unfamiliar customs and outmoded science, they are entering the presence of the living God and are themselves a part of its drama and unfolding purpose. Because they want their children to grow into this same knowledge, they welcome the help of the church school. Coleridge said that the Bible was the book which found him most readily. It can find children. As they paint in response to its stories, they learn the truth about themselves, their world, and God. Moreover, the distinctive art of the Hebrew storyteller was born of intense conviction and feeling expressed with great simplicity in the language of poetry, a language that children understand intuitively and with which they feel at home. Poetry came before prose in the history of creative writing, and young children do not have to analyze symbolic imagery to catch its meaning. The stories of Adam and Eve, of Noah, or the crossing of the Red Sea speak directly to them if we do not intrude our own adult problems of interpretation.

Questions will be asked in good time, but should not be imposed nor stimulated prematurely, nor on any account discussed at the time of painting. Whatever interpretation is necessary should be thought through with the children in advance. For example, the important thing in the Garden of Eden story is not the mechanics of the serpent's language, but how eager Adam and Eve were (as are all of us) to do as they pleased and blame someone else when they were caught. In the story of Jonah the real issue is not how he could stay alive for three days inside a whale, but how amazingly God's concern for the welfare of everybody pushed even the grudging Jonah to bear a message of hope to the wicked people of Ninevah, and how (to his surprise and disappointment!) they actually began to mend their ways.

To catch the ear of children subjected to the highly charged emotions of television, stories about matters of life and death are more successful above the preschool age than those about Billy riding a bicycle on his birthday. The protectiveness which once rejected the use of a Bible story containing sin and suffering denied to children an important part of their foundation for a sturdy faith. Moses killing the Egyptian or David conniving to liquidate Uriah were frowned on because they showed heroes to be imperfect. In a world-wide meeting of Christian educators after the Second World War, a young man from Holland, who had been active in the resistance movement during the Nazi occupation, said that what he most needed to hear was not a story of perfect men but of someone like David, who had sinned and yet was not abandoned by God. He did not mean to condone evil but to make a plea that the Church teach grace rather than moralism. Naturally we would not tell all the details of every story to children, but they have a right to know that when they have done wrong, they are not unique and that God will not forsake them. Since that long-ago meeting, however, educators have also come to see that behavior does have to be held in direct relationship to grace in order to see if the grace we claim is active in our lives.

Our world is dangerous, and this fact cannot be hidden, but it can be related to a faith that is adequate for living in such a world. Martin Buber saw the need for such faith in Germany as the Nazis came to power. He saw Jewish education as a form of spiritual resistance: "The children see what is happening and are silent," he said. "The world has become unsafe. What is to be done? I know nothing else but this: to bring something unshakable into the world of the child. . . ." [2] An unshakable faith was passed on to the ancient Hebrews in stories around the campfire. We must make sure we pass such a faith on to our children today.

The story of David's battle with Goliath is an example of strong faith. David was the little fellow up against the big one, but because his religion was more real to him than to any other person there, including the king, he was willing to risk everything to challenge the power of evil. He believed that God was God. The others accepted the logic of Goliath and were defeated without even trying. It is interesting to know that some playgrounds in Scandinavia and in England are designed with natural settings that provide opportunity for danger and risk, the theory being that a fallen tree across a "ravine" or a jagged rock to climb can stimulate more courage than conventional equipment. To their objectors, the modern designers say, "Better a broken arm than a broken spirit."

Fear is as much our enemy in the space age as pride is. It results in a rattling of national sabers, and it disturbs our children's dreams. We must let them hear the thunder of the Biblical themes again and again so that it will penetrate to the core of their being as they paint their response to the God who not only creates, but who surely rescues, restores, and fulfills. Abraham leaving his home for good because God told him to; Moses, the stammerer, leading a nation out of slavery; Joseph forgiving his brothers who had tried to kill him, even letting them have food to save their lives; Jeremiah despised by Jerusalem for telling the truth; Jerusalem destroyed but built again by Nehemiah; Jesus making his commitment in Gethsemane, dying on the Cross but restored to us in the Resurrection. This *is* our Father's world, and no matter how dark the moment, all creation moves toward his *ultimate* victory. To quote from a sermon by Dr. Robert J. McCracken, of Riverside Church, ". . . the end of it all is a resurrection and not a burial, a festival and not a funeral. . . ."

The theme of reconciliation encompasses all the stories of service, sacrifice, and forgiveness; the relationships of obedience and disobedience, of fellowship and devotion; the warnings of prophets; the truths of the Parables; the faith of disciple and saint, missionary hero and martyr for freedom. Although a major portion of the subject matter used in church schools may be Biblical, the later history of the Church and of how the Bible came to be also provide dramatic and significant material.

Great riches are to be found in stories of the Middle Ages and the Reformation, in the lives of the composers of great church music, missionaries, and the writers of hymns. Colorful associations come to mind: the Crusades, cathedrals, St. Francis, brother of the birds, Wycliffe and Tyndale, Martin Luther, Johann Sebastian Bach, Father Damien, missionary to lepers. In our own time there are the men and women like Marian Anderson and Martin Luther King, Jr., who have a dream for today and tomorrow.

One of the richest mines of material for painting can be found through a study of the great cathedrals, the architecture of joy. To know them is to know the heart and mind and faith and the great art of the Middle Ages. In their stained-glass windows alone there is a veritable library of Christian history, biography, legend, and symbolism. In her beautiful little book, *Singing Windows,* Mary Young gives a clear and accurate account of the part artists played in building the cathedrals, and tells where some of the famous windows can be found in America, as well as in Europe (notably in the Washington Cathedral and in the Cathedral Church St. John the Divine in New York). Juniors and older primaries will enjoy the book as well as their teachers.

Art was related to faith not only through architecture and music and painting, but also in the effort to keep the Bible alive during the Dark Ages. It was the monks who made copies of the Scriptures, working by candlelight during the long winter months, decorating the parchments with exquisite designs and miniatures called illuminations. There is a charming story about a copyist in the book *Castle, Abbey and Town,* by Irma Simonton Black. Although "Brother Louis" was not engaged in copying the Bible, the story provides an excellent understanding of the spirit in which the monks went about their task. In fact, the little book will "illuminate" the entire period of the Middle Ages for juniors preparing to respond through creative art to that period of Christian history.

For convenient reference, Biblical material which can stimulate good painting is listed in the Appendix. The stories are related to the three Biblical themes of Creation, Reconciliation, and Fulfillment. The themes are not mutually exclusive, of course, any more than the ceaseless activity of God in bestowing, freeing, and fulfilling life is split up in separate compartments. Jesus' birth and the birth of the Church are a part of creation, for example, and they are also acts of reconciliation and fulfillment. The hymns mentioned can help inspire painting by their imagery and feeling, or enrich its meaning later, especially if they are sung by the children in unison. They have a triple strand of interest: the composer, the writer, and their imagery.

A brief look at one story, that of Isaiah in the Temple, will help to reveal the dynamic relationship of event and theme, of knowledge and emotion: Isaiah knew the facts of his country's danger when he went into the Temple; he knew that the military might of Assyria was moving nearer and nearer the little countries of Israel and Judah, and he was gravely concerned for their survival. While in the house of worship, he has a vision which brings him into the very presence of God . . . holy, holy, holy! This fills him with a sense of his own sinfulness and that of the entire nation, but his cry of despair is answered by the cleansing fire brought by the seraphim from the altar. It is only then that Isaiah hears God's call to service, and only then that he can respond, "Send me." This story illustrates the themes of giving and renewing life, and the foundation for the theme of fulfillment which came later when the Assyrians were driven back. The story also illustrates faith and commitment. Junior children can know all of this, but it is best when such knowledge is already theirs before the day of painting. In preparing them through the story for the immediate moment of creative expression, it is the sense of the holy we must try to help them feel, and the vivid imagery of relationship we must help them see, not at this point telling them in so many words, but telling them through our own feeling of awe as we present the story, and our own vivid picture of the cry, the cleansing fire, the call from God, and Isaiah's offering of himself.

For beginning teachers, examples are given below that may be useful as a guide in preparing their own introductions or background before the children paint:

The Red Sea Crossing (Exodus 14:10-30): "The people of Israel have just passed through one danger only to be faced by another. After Pharaoh finally agreed to let them go, Moses led them to the edge of the wilderness where they made camp near the sea for the night. Suddenly they learn that Pharaoh's mighty army is coming after them and is now rapidly approaching. They are coming nearer and nearer. What are they going to do?" (The story proper begins now, at verse 10.)

Jesus Stills the Storm (Mark 4:35-41): "Near the Sea of Galilee there is a mountain called Mt. Hermon where the snow never melts. Without warning, cold air rushes down from the mountain onto the Sea of Galilee below and blows up sudden storms. This happened one evening back in Jesus' day when he and the disciples were sailing across the lake. Let's see what happened." (Begin the story at verse 35.)

The same basic truths presented in the Bible and expressed in the history of the Church and other vehicles of God's activity continue to break through so that our subject matter is derived not only from our inheritance but also from what God is doing in the world today. This includes us and the children we teach. When our work together is creative, it will be more like a tapestry than a straight line, a tapestry woven of many ideas and feelings and activities as life is. A group can begin anywhere in subject matter, with a personal experience, a game, a picture, acting out a poem or a song, or listening to a story of understanding. Perhaps a conviction will emerge leading to some sacrificial action, for seeing through the eyes of an artist in any field helps children see more clearly through the eyes of Christ, and, conversely, the more they understand him as he moves through the life of the New Testament and their own lives, the better they will paint.

It is not possible or desirable to paint everything. Many daily experiences are not dramatic enough to motivate painting and are more suitable for conversation or creative writing. Moreover, children are likely to paint subjects from daily life at school, and repetition will not stimulate growth or new insights. When a teacher is convinced that a child is working in a rut, she must encourage him to get out of it. In fact, there is so little time to give children all that is awaiting their discovery in the Bible, and that is insistently relevant to their everyday life, that one may hesitate to spend time on other subject matter until he knows it must be done to bring together for the children the realities of the past and present.

Sometimes children enjoy consciously trying to paint feelings. Lines, color, and shapes can be combined to suggest jealousy, hate, anger, love, or happiness. A brief tryout period is a good time to explore this kind of subject matter. It is wise not to spend an entire hour painting negative feelings at this age, for if a child is burdened by them in reality, they are likely to be confirmed rather than released. If he is not so burdened, the painting is a mere exercise and not worth doing for a full session. It is more wholesome to paint from an interesting subject which will bring about release of tension unconsciously without concentrating on it.

Young primaries are fond of little things like puppies, chipmunks, or a butterfly. They like to hold and feel a smooth pebble from the beach, a twig of pine, a patch of green velvet moss. When they bring their nature offerings to the Wonder Table to be shared and enjoyed, they may want to tell how they found them. If there is a surge of feeling, it can be expressed in a song or prayer of praise or creative movement. Later all this can be related to Jesus' love for the little as well as the big, his respect for the simple and the unpretentious. How he blessed the children and admired the flowers of the field can be the subject for a conversation, and one of the stories Jesus himself told of the widow's mite, the lost sheep, the lost coin, or the tiny mustard seed which grew up to shelter the birds of the air can be woven into the pattern. The time to paint may come at any point along the way, and the better we know the children, the more certain we will be of that moment when it comes.

Dramatic qualities appeal to children of all six elementary grades, and the younger ones can prepare for painting by a short pantomime of a story or the lines of a hymn, or an original creative movement of the kind Natalie Robinson Cole describes in *The Arts in the Classroom*. Older children can prepare through role plays, or they can plan a dialogue for scenes they want to dramatize; both provide rich inspiration for painting.[3] Dramatic action is plentiful in the stories of Ruth and Naomi, Joseph and his brothers, the Good Samaritan, the Cleansing of the Temple, or St. Paul's escape over the Damascus wall—all favorite subjects with juniors. Richard, a nine-year-old, took keen delight in painting the overturned tables of the money-changers and the doves zooming like airplanes into the wide blue yonder.

Children are fascinated by the idea of a journey, and they can paint from one of their own or from one of the many in the Bible: how Abraham left home with his family and all their possessions to go to a new and strange place; how Joseph was transported as a slave to Egypt, quite possibly tied to the back of a donkey; the heartbreaking trek of the Hebrews from Jerusalem to their exile in Babylonia; the three journeys of Mary and Joseph; the storms at sea in Jonah and the Book of Acts.

Since children are a part of what we teach, and simply because we love them, we want to know something about them and the circumstances of their lives, their happiness, hardship, deprivation, or abundance, their fears and hopes. It is hard to come by this kind of knowledge unless a teacher has contacts with their families in addition to Sunday morning. Calling in the home is especially helpful—even if only once a year in each child's home. If both parents work, are tired at night and sleep on Sundays, it will be difficult to arrange. Some teachers ask parents to choose a time best for them to come to the church for a conference. One director has done her part by holding open office one night each week for both teachers and parents to drop in and get acquainted. In order to be with the children of her class more often, one teacher has held a birthday party at the church each month, another likes to invite the children, two at a time, to be her guests for dinner. By such means will the leading question a teacher asks herself become more meaningful: What is the gospel, the good news, for these particular children at this particular time?

In some groups there will be children who have had little or no opportunity for previous religious instruction, others for whom the association has not been entirely attractive. "Jesus Christ" may mean swearing to one, a sissy to another. Here and there someone with the best intention may have inoculated a child against Bible stories by moralizing, or by telling them in a sacred tone of voice, or by illustrating them with pallid, sentimental pictures, none of which relate to real life as the children know it. They should not be scolded when they rebel. "Do we have to hear that stuff again?" is a hint, straight from those who know, that a new approach is called for, and the teacher can be guided by it gratefully, searching for ways to build new images.

Without preaching, she can tell the story of the storm when the disciples panicked and Jesus kept calm; or she can open a discussion on carpentry, the muscle it takes to carry wood and saw it, the skill required to make a heavy yoke for oxen. It could be a revealing experience for a group of boys to visit a modern carpenter shop and then be provided with one in their own church where they could learn firsthand that carpentry is no work for a weakling. Children can also learn to respect Jesus' ability to walk long distances between towns, for he had no car to make him soft. His gift for telling stories attracted crowds of men, women, and children, who followed him about to listen and learn how to live, and it is thrilling for children to know they can hear some of the same stories he told.

Open-end stories are an excellent way to involve children in a lively discussion of problems they might meet in their own lives. These stories are left unfinished so that children can think through in each case how the problem might be solved and the story completed. Out of the heated exchange this procedure can generate, good painting can come as well as insights in practical Christianity and a deeper acquaintance with the teacher. Each child can write or tell his own version of how the story should end and then express it in painting, or the picture may be the child's response to the story as a whole rather than an illustration for the final scene. The Seabury curriculum is an excellent resource for such material. There is also a recording of two open-end stories produced by the Methodist Church for the primary material in the Asbury Series. Some teachers like to arrange an unfinished story themselves, using, of course, material unfamiliar to the children. This can make an exciting project for a department to undertake.

Stories of "attitude" are favorites among children, although they may not know them by that term. They are really character-building stories, but subtly so, with plenty of action or humor to carry the concept. Some of Aesop's fables belong in this category, and even the uproarious books of Dr. Seuss, although one hesitates to say so for fear of spoiling the fun. *Make Way for Ducklings* teaches love and consideration for animals most delightfully as the policeman on the corner holds up traffic for the little brood to cross the street. Eleanor Farjeon's *Mrs. Malone* shares the joy of believing there is always room for one more even in a humble cottage. Hans Christian Andersen's *Ugly Duckling* is a story of sheer grace. His story about the Emperor's new clothes is really an extension of "Except ye become as a little child," and *The Swineherd* lets us know what happens to a princess who puts material things first. "Where your heart is, there will your treasure be." There are many stories of courage, notably of men of science and space today or of people like Charles Lindbergh or Columbus. Alice Dalgliesh has written stories about both, and Enid Meadowcroft's *Ship Boy with Columbus* lets us live with a lad on Columbus' voyage of discovery. In *Ride on the Wind,* Miss Dalgliesh retells for children the story of the *Spirit of St. Louis.* It has everything: earth and sky, the vastness of the sea, Lindbergh's loneliness and the temptation to sleep (which would have been fatal), a prayer for strength to carry him through, and gratitude for the stars which helped to guide him on the long flight.

A story such as this, showing what it costs to be the first to attempt the impossible, can lead us back full circle to thinking about Jesus again. In what way was he a pioneer? In what way was his "first" the same as Lindbergh's or John Glenn's? In what way different? Who *was* Jesus? Let the children talk and and ask and paint, and hopefully, they will feel it a privilege to learn more of him. They may enjoy seeing a print of Rembrandt's "Christ with the Sick, Receiving Little Children," for it is a luminous statement by a great artist of what being in Christ's presence means. Through it we may see that the only distance between us and God is the difference between us and Christ.

One day while walking in a busy neighborhood, I saw a sign outside a church: "Jesus Christ died for our sins and rose again on the third day. Will tell you more about this next week." I wondered whether many would come to listen. There was a crowd when Peter preached at Pentecost, but something had happened to make those words meaningful. Perhaps something was happening in this church now to make the words a living creed. The members may already have opened their hearts and their doors to the people of the neighborhood, who may already have begun to understand the resurrection from the dead. Important as real images of Jesus are, children also need a true image of the Church to find their own true likeness.

The Relationship of Themes

The basic elements of subject matter in Christian education should be maintained continuously in dynamic relation to each other. A brief outline is given below as a reminder of our purpose and involvement.

1. Basic Biblical Themes

   Creation: God is the Creator; we are his creatures.

   Separation (sin): The creature wants to be God and breaks the true relationship even when he knows the wonder of it.

   Reconciliation (brought together again): In his steadfast love, God searches for his children until they are found and restored, regardless of the cost.

   Fulfillment: This has already happened in Jesus Christ, continues to happen through him, but is not yet perfected.[4] (See Appendix for the expanded list of themes and their relevant Bible stories and hymns.)

2. The Life of Christ

3. The Story of the Church

4. The Child and His Daily Life

   The Child: his ambitions, attitudes, beliefs, feelings.

   Neighborhood (city? town? country?): home, school, church, synagogue, park, playground.

   People: family, friends, neighbors, teachers, ministers, rabbis, priests, postman, policemen.

   Pleasant things: birthdays, games, music, pets, playmates, vacations.

   Hard things: a broken home, being laughed at, death, discrimination, failure, fighting a bully, going hungry, mistreatment, labor strikes, poverty.

   Puzzling things: Why are things the way they are? Why can't I do as I please? Why did my father (or mother) desert us? Where do you go when you die? What is God like? What is the difference between God and Jesus? How come I feel two ways about the same person? Quarreling and making up.

Taking responsibility: being on time, helping Dad and Mother, playing fair, practicing my music, doing home-work, sharing something I'd like to keep, doing a service for someone, obeying rules, telling the truth.

5. The Teacher

Whatever happens in the teacher's daily life, whoever she is as a person, will be a part of the subject matter she teaches whether she is aware of it or not.

CHAPTER 10

USING RESOURCES
EFFECTIVELY

Including art does not automatically produce creative teaching. To stimulate imagination and bring about growth and change in both teacher and child it is essential to have inter-relatedness of ideas as well as people. This is why knowledge of resources is important. Music, pictures, poems, rhythms can all contribute to creative painting, as can trips and conversations. During a unit that might be called "Who Am I?" for example, primary children will enjoy the poetry in *Me,* by Inez Hogan, and the storybook *Just Me,* by Marie Hall Ets. To lead up to the Genesis story of creation, a "beauty walk," one of the films from the God's Wonders series, or Rachel Carson's book *A Sense of Wonder* can be stimulating. After the story comes the painting, and, after that, children can see Paul Galdone's illustrations in *The First Seven Days* or go to a museum to see a great painting of flowers, a rainbow, or the sea, or a portrait by Rembrandt. If no museum is accessible, the teacher can show color prints in the classroom. Whatever preparation helps children to know God will be good as long-term preparation for painting. The richer this preparation is, the better. Children can respond to a story of Biblical truth with no previous knowledge of the heritage, without previous experience in the church, and even without having been loved before, but, as is the case with any pursuit, those who are both informed and experienced can respond with more of themselves. If children have known joy and acceptance, have joined in corporate worship, have dramatized a story, have listened to a psalm and learned it, have sung a hymn and prayed together, have located Jesus' home village on a map (and know how to spell it!), have heard a returned traveler describe his visit to Jerusalem, have been cherished in the warmth of fellowship, then their minds and spirits will be richly furnished with a religious vision which can join hands with art. The symbols and the bursts of color in Chagall's Jerusalem windows were not accidents. His Jewish heritage had given him a knowledge of the Bible and a feeling for the Hebrew faith which his ability as an artist could express. As for the children, when they have objectified through art the truths they have been learning, they are not likely to forget them.

It is suggested that whoever teaches painting in the church school carry file cards or a notebook on which to jot down ideas worth passing along to the children. Perhaps a book in a shop window will catch the eye, or a picture in a gallery, or on a magazine cover; or there may be a "happening" to recall. These cards can be handy during a visit of discovery to a library. For example, here are notes on David taken from Fleming James' *Personalities of the Old Testament*:

Reigned 1016-976 B.C. brought Israel to its zenith. O.T. narrative at its best, yet dominated by God's love in action. . . . Dynasty lasted 400 years. . . . Bible source: Samuel I and II, I Kings, 1 and 2. "No more romantic story is to be found in the world's literature than that of the shepherd boy of Bethlehem who won a king's favour, then lost it and became a hunted outlaw, only to be made king himself . . . then sinned deeply and saw nemesis work itself out in his house till he died a broken-hearted old man in the midst of the splendour he had created. . . ." (p. 119)

And notes on Nehemiah from the twenty-third chapter of the same source:

Active in Judah about 445-432 B.C. Despair in the Jewish community in Jerusalem. . . . demoralized. . . . walls and gates still in ruins. . . . strong leadership needed. . . . Nehemiah, the wine-bearer to the King of Persia, hears the news. . . . takes the risk. . . . asks king's favor to return and help his people. Granted. . . . a big thing to leave comfort and safety, travel back to hard work and danger. . . . Many local enemies. . . . secret ride at midnight around the walls to see what can be done. . . . people rally to the task. . . . a triumphal procession of thanksgiving on top of the re-built walls. . . . to the temple. . . . musicians, chanting, women, children, cymbals, harps. . . .

Notes from the fifth chapter of *The Hidden Years,* by John Oxenham, an imaginary account of Jesus' boyhood and youth presented with authentic background and spirit:

Jesus and his friend Azor stretch out on hillside to watch heavy traffic on the Great Road below. Camels swaying with heavy packs, the smell of spices, herds of cattle and oxen, flocks of bleating sheep, Roman soldiers marching. Carts pass, loaded with wild beasts for the games in Rome. Cattle frightened, beasts roar. *Azor:* "They are always hungry." *Jesus:* "It is hard for them." . . . Important personage moves up in chariot (could be King Herod). Trumpets, slaves, more soldiers. Wayfarers rudely scattered and pushed off road. Jesus frowns, tight-lipped, kicks ground behind him.

Some of the material in this fascinating book might be re-told in modern style, but many scenes can be read aloud just as they are. Children especially appreciate the story of how Jesus hurled a boy to the ground because he was torturing a little dog. Then, Jesus carried the half-dead animal home to care for him even though dogs were not greatly respected in those days and few would have wanted one for a pet. Or the one about the swimming pond where Jesus saved from drowning a boy who became frightened and began to sink. Talking with his friend afterward, Jesus wondered why swimming seemed as easy as running to him. "You do not know fear," his friend replied, but Jesus was not quite satisfied with this because he remembered that he had felt very much afraid when he saw the boy going under. "That was different," his friend replied, "You were afraid for him, not for yourself." This episode has a punch line, for the boy whom Jesus saved was the same one he had seen abusing the dog.

Through this story, children might come to talk about their own fears, discover each other more deeply, and gain a less limiting idea of Jesus as well as greater freedom for themselves. Books are legion that help relate children to the content of the church school curriculum: John W. Flight's classic on Moses, Margaret Dulles Edwards' *Child of the Sun* (the story of the pharaoh Akhenaten), the Anglund books on special ways of feeling, Sheila Burnford's story of courage in *The Incredible Journey,* others of wonder, humility, or grace. Meindert DeJong has given us books for children with both dreams and realism, not only in the reference book *Bible Days,* so helpful to young children, but also in his satisfying stories of everyday life. When in search of supplementary material sure to be well done, teachers can browse through the Caldecott or Newberry annual award books or the bibliographies of books on storytelling.

The following resources provide opportunities to discover treasures that may have been unknown before.

Books

Art

Alexander, Cecil, *All Things Bright and Beautiful.* New York: Charles Scribner's Sons, 1962. A hymn for children, illustrated by Leo Politi.

Away in a Manger. New York: Thomas Nelson & Sons, World Council of Churches and Sunday School Association, 1963.

"The Bible," *Life* Magazine, December 25, 1964. A special issue on the Bible and the art it has inspired. Biblical interpretations by scholars, illustrations from great religious art.

Brown, Margaret Wise. *The Color Kittens*. New York: The Golden Press, n.d. Lively kittens learn about colors and how to mix them with their paint brushes. (First Grade or Under.)

Freund, Miriam, *Jewels for a Crown*. New York: The McGraw-Hill Book Company, 1963. The story of the Jerusalem windows by Chagall, illustrated in color.

The Life of Christ. Institute of Arts of the City of Detroit; Detroit, Michigan. A beautiful booklet illustrated with prints of the great masterpieces at the Institute.

In Our Image. Illustrated by Guy Rowe. New York: Oxford University Press, 1949. Portraits of the Prophets. Rather stark.

Spilke, Arnold, *Paint All Kinds of Pictures*. New York: Henry Z. Walck, 1963. Inspiration for painting "feeling" pictures. Illustrations express feelings that are scary, funny, gay, exciting, quiet, "loud," and so forth.

Wahl, Jean, *Illustrations for the Bible*. New York: Harcourt, Brace & Company, 1956. Striking illustrations by Marc Chagall.

Weisgard, Leonard, *Treasures to See*. New York: Harcourt, Brace & World, 1956. An introduction to museumgoing. (Grades 1-4.)

The Bible

Allstrom, Elizabeth, *Songs Along the Way*. New York: Abingdon Press, 1964. Selected psalms with helpful background comment. Illustrated with woodcuts of authentic spirit.

Angland, Joan Walsh, *A Book of Good Tidings*. New York: Harcourt, Brace & World, 1965. Verses from the Bible in another enchanting book illustrated by the author.

Bassage, Harold (ed.), *God and His People*. New York: The Seabury Press, 1966. The Old Testament story of God's dealings with his people and their response to him, told in the language of the King James Version, arranged for readability in the manner of verse. Illustrations by a noted sculptor, Clark Fitz-Gerald. (Older Junior.)

Bible Readings for Boys and Girls. New York: Thomas Nelson
& Sons, 1959. Selections from the Revised Standard Version.
Beautifully illustrated by Lynd Ward. (Junior.)

Duncan, Cleo, *Woofy Is Forgiven* and *The Prodigal Son.* Boston: United Church Press, 1964. A charming story for primary children about a family of bears. Clarifies the meaning
of a simplified version of the Prodigal Son, which follows.

Edwards, Margaret D., *Child of the Sun:* A Pharaoh of Egypt.
Boston: Beacon Press, 1939.

A First Bible. Selected and arranged by Jean Maury. New York:
Henry Z. Walck, 1934. Based on the King James Version;
illustrated by Helen Sewell.

Flight, John W., *Moses: Egyptian Prince, Nomad, Sheikh, Law-
giver.* Boston: Beacon Press, 1942.

———— *The Drama of Ancient Israel.* Boston: Beacon Press,
1949.

Heiderstadt, Dorothy, *To All Nations.* New York: Thomas Nelson & Sons, 1959. How the Bible was made available to the
common people. Includes stories of Wycliffe, Tyndale,
Luther, Judson, and others. (Junior.)

Hollender, Betty, *Bible Stories for Little Children,* Book 3. New
York: The American Hebrew Congregation, 1960. These
stories, which are retold, include Amos, Elijah, Hosea,
Isaiah, Jeremiah, Nehemiah, Jonah, and others.

Northcott, Cecil, *Bible Encyclopedia for Children.* Philadelphia: The Westminster Press, 1964. Interesting and richly
informative; nondenominational. Both design and illustrations are imaginative and colorful. Will be enjoyed by
adults too.

Oxenham, John, *The Hidden Years.* New York: David McKay,
1958 reprint. A classic; it reconstructs the times during
which Jesus lived and presents an imagined account of his
boyhood and youth about which the Bible is largely silent.

Shippen, Katherine, *Moses.* New York: Harper & Brothers,
1949.

Smither, Ethel, *Early Old Testament Stories.* New York: Abingdon Press, 1954. Abraham, Jacob, Joseph, Moses.

———— *Later Old Testament Stories*. New York: Abingdon Press, 1956. Ruth, David, Solomon, Naboth, Nehemiah.

Towers, Grace Storm, *A Journey into Time*. Boston: United Church Press, 1963. A short story of modern children visiting in Palestine is followed by others about children who lived there centuries ago. Brings the Biblical background alive in a personal way, both accurate and exciting. (Junior.)

Winants, Miche, *Noah's Ark*. New York: Harcourt, Brace & World, 1965. Unusual illustrations by the author.

Young Readers Bible. Philadelphia: A. J. Holman Company (for Cokesbury), 1965. An unabridged study edition of the Revised Standard Version with interpretive material. (Older Junior and Up.)

Zacharias, Alfred, *The Babylonian Dragon*. Philadelphia: Muhlenberg Press, 1961. Contains five stories based on the Old Testament and illustrating the idea that the Bible is not always serious and sober. "Listening between the lines we can hear the angels laugh." Older Junior; Teachers.)

The Church

Agnew, Edith J., *People of the Way*. Philadelphia: The Westminster Press, 1959. The story of the Early Church. (Primary.)

Bainton, Roland, *The Church of Our Fathers*. Philadelphia: The Westminster Press, 1950.

Bowie, Walter Russell, *The Story of the Church*. New York: Abingdon Press, 1955.

Busoni, Rafaello, *Somi Builds a Church*. New York: The Viking Press, 1943. A miracle of faith in northern Norway as Somi and his son, with a group of Laps, build a church at great cost and sacrifice.

Hummel, Ruth, *Little Martin Luther*. St. Louis, Mo.: Concordia Publishing House, 1962. (Junior.)

Lillie, Amy Morris, *I Will Build My Church*. Philadelphia: The Westminster Press, 1950. (Junior.)

McGowen, Drusilla, *The Church Grows.* Two stories for juniors about the Early Church. Part of the Episcopal Church Curriculum. New York: The Seabury Press, 1964.

McNeer, May, *Martin Luther.* New York: Abingdon Press, 1953. (Junior.)

Smither, Ethel, *First to Be Called Christians.* New York: Abingdon Press, 1955.

Spratt, Barnett, *Toppy and the Circuit Rider.* New York: Abingdon Press, 1957. (Older Primary and Junior.)

Tower, Grace, *Pioneers of the Church.* Philadelphia: United Church Press, 1964. From Antioch pioneers to modern children. (Junior.)

Trickey, Edna, *Billy Finds Out.* Philadelphia: United Church Press, 1964. Everyday life in relation to the Church.

Creation

And It Was So. Illustrated by Tasha Tudor. Philadelphia: The Westminster Press, 1958. (Primary.)

The First Seven Days. Illustrated by Paul Galdone. New York: Thomas Y. Crowell, 1962. An inspiring presentation of the story of creation from Genesis. (Primary or Junior.)

Hickson, Agnes, *God the Creator.* Part of the Episcopal Curriculum. New York: The Seabury Press, 1964. (First Grade.)

Creative Rhythm

Andrews, Gladys, *Creative Rhythmic Movement for Children.* Englewood Cliffs, N.J.: Prentice-Hall, 1954.

Cole, Natalie Robinson, *The Arts in the Classroom.* New York: John Day Company, 1940.

LaSalle, Dorothy, *Rhythms and Dances for Elementary School.* New York: The Ronald Press, 1951.

Taylor, Margaret Fisk, *Time for Wonder.* Philadelphia: Christian Education Press, 1961.

The Inner City

Archibald, Helen, *Good News.* The Chicago City Missionary Society, 19 LaSalle Street, Chicago, Illinois 60603. A curriculum for children of the inner city written while the author was working in the East Harlem Protestant Parish.

Cole, Natalie Robinson, *The Arts in the Classroom.* New York: John Day Company, 1940. Useful suggestions on creative writing and rhythms as well as on painting, for the inner city.

Keats, Ezra Jack, *John Henry, an American Legend.* New York: Pantheon Books, 1965. A dramatic story of railroad building, featuring a young Negro as hero. Should help Negro children reinforce their sense of dignity and worth.

Lewis, Richard W., *A Summer Adventure.* New York: Harper & Row, 1962. A well-written story about a Negro boy on a farm who faces some basic questions about life through his interest in animals. Should be read by all city children for understanding of country life.

Lorstand, Joseph A., *Call Them Heroes.* Morristown, N.J.: Silver Burdette Company, 1965. (Junior.) This paperback contains true stories, simply but powerfully written by the Deputy Superintendent of Schools in New York City, based on interviews with successful citizens from meager backgrounds on the Lower East Side who did NOT drop out of school. All ethnic groups are represented, although many of the profiles are of Puerto Ricans and Negroes. Illustrated by photographs of the subjects.

Palmer, Candida, *Snow Storm Before Christmas.* Philadelphia: J. B. Lippincott, 1965. Two inner-city Negro children go shopping for Christmas and are caught in a snow storm. (Primary.)

A Teacher's Notebook of Negro History and Culture. Compiled by Helen Archibald. Available from the Chicago City Missionary Society. Will help develop a Negro child's sense of identity and significance, and should be read by children of other races to enlarge their understanding.

Jesus Christ

Fosdick, Harry Emerson, *Jesus of Nazareth.* New York: Random House, 1959. (Upper Junior.)

Savage, Carol, *The Lord Jesus.* Part of the Episcopal Church Curriculum. New York: The Seabury Press, 1954. (Primary.)

Smart, James D., *Jesus, Stories for Children.* Philadelphia: The Westminster Press, 1949. (Primary.)

The Son of God. New York: The Seabury Press, 1957. Readings from the Gospel according to St. Mark, with background information by Edric A. Weld and William Sydnor. Part of the Episcopal Curriculum. (Older Junior.)

Smither, Ethel, *Stories of Jesus.* New York: Abingdon Press, 1954. Among others, includes stories of Zacchaeus, the Prodigal Son, and the Good Samaritan.

The Middle Ages (Approximately 500–1500)

Black, Irma Simonton, *Castle, Abbey and Town.* New York: Holiday House, 1963. How people lived, including the story of Brother Louis, a monk who copied manuscripts (pp. 59ff.).

Langford, Norman, *Fire Upon the Earth.* Part of the United Presbyterian Curriculum. Philadelphia: The Westminster Press, 1950. Part II: The Church Becomes an Empire. (Upper Junior.)

Malcomson, Anne, *Miracle Plays.* Boston: Houghton Mifflin Company, 1959. Includes "The Statue of St. Nicholas" and others.

Time, The Weekly Newsmagazine, "Manuscripts," December 25, 1964, page 40.

Young, Mary, *Singing Windows.* New York: Abingdon Press, 1962. The history of stained glass, work of the artists, legends, and information on which cathedrals have some of the famous windows.

Missionaries

Fox, Genevieve, *Sir Wilfred Grenfell.* New York: Thomas Y. Crowell, 1942. A lively account of the young English doctor who became a missionary in Labrador. (Junior.)

Heiderstadt, Dorothy, *To All Nations*. New York: Thomas Nelson & Sons, 1959.

Missionary Story Hour, compiled by Nina Millen. New York: Friendship Press, 1952.

Roos, Ann, *Man of Molokai*. Philadelphia: J. B. Lippincott Company, 1943. A well-written story of Father Damien, missionary to lepers. (Junior.)

See also various books of the Friendship Press, New York City.

Music

Bonner, Clint, *A Hymn Is Born*. Nashville: Broadman Press, 1959.

Britten, Benjamin, and Holst, Imogen, *Wonderful World of Music*. New York: Doubleday & Company, 1958.

Einstein, Alfred, *A Short History of Music*. New York: Alfred A. Knopf, 1947.

McCutcheon, Robert, *Our Hymnody*. New York: Abingdon Press, n.d.

Thomas, Edith Lovell, *Music in Christian Education*. New York: Abingdon Press, 1953.

Wheeler, Opal, *Bach, the Boy of Thuringia*. New York: E. P. Dutton & Company, 1937. (Junior.)

Hymnbooks

Sing for Joy. Compiled by Norman and Margaret Mealy. New York: The Seabury Press, 1961.

Songs and Hymns for Primary Worship. Philadelphia: The Westminster Press, 1964.

The Hymnal 1940. New York: The [Protestant Episcopal] Church Pension Fund.

The Pilgrim Hymnal. Boston: Pilgrim Press, 1958.

Songs of Many Nations. Delaware, Ohio: Cooperative Recreation Service, 1958. (Folk Songs, Rounds, Fun Songs.)

Poetry

Aldis, Dorothy, *Everything and Anything*. New York: Pantheon

Books, 1956. Contains the charming poem "Little," among others.

—— *Hello, Day.* New York: G. P. Putnam's Sons, 1959. Contains "My Brother."

Away We Go! Compiled by Catherine McEwen. New York: Thomas Y. Crowell, 1956. One hundred poems, including several on the city about bridges, traffic lights, and escalators. (Primary.)

Becker, John, *New Feathers for the Old Goose.* New York: Pantheon Books, 1956. Includes the delightful "Feather or Fur."

The Birds and the Beasts Were There. Selected by William Cole. Cleveland: World Publishing Company, 1963. (Primary.)

Ciardi, John, *The Reason for the Pelican.* Philadelphia: J. B. Lippincott Company, 1959. "Someone" is about birthdays.

Hammond, Penny, and Thomas, Katrina, *My Skyscraper City.* New York: Doubleday & Company, 1963. Charming photographs illustrate appropriate verses for this "child's view" of New York.

Hogan, Inez, *Me.* New York: E. P. Dutton & Company, 1954. Simple poems for everyday, helpful for self-discovery. (Primary.)

A Pocketful of Rhymes. Edited by Katherine Love. New York: Thomas Y. Crowell, 1946. Includes poems by James Stephens, Vachel Lindsay, Walter de la Mare. (Primary or Junior.)

Rasmussen, Carrie, *Let's Say Poetry Together and Have Fun.* Minneapolis: Burgess Publishing Company, 1963. One hundred and fifty poems arranged for choral reading.

Seuss, Dr., *I Had Trouble in Getting to Solla Sollew.* New York: Random House, 1965. Fantastic humor every child will enjoy. (Primary.)

This Way, Delight. Poems selected by Herbert Read. New York: Pantheon Books, 1956. Not written especially for children but will interest advanced juniors. Has a wide range including Kipling, Dickinson, Eliot. Herbert Read, himself a poet and critic, has written an "afterthought," instead of an introduction, in which he encourages the reader to try writing poetry too.

A Way of Knowing. Compiled by Gerald McDonald. New York: Thomas Y. Crowell, 1959. A collection of poems for boys, including T. S. Eliot's "Macavity: The Mystery Cat," and others about swimming, slot machines, and the zoo. (Junior.)

Prayer

Farjeon, Eleanor, *Prayer for Little Things.* Boston: Houghton Mifflin Company, 1945.

Hogan, Bernice, *Now I Lay Me Down to Wonder.* New York: Abingdon Press, 1961. (First Grade.)

Our Prayers and Praise. Morning Prayer, Holy Communion, and Collects, from the Book of Common Prayer. New York: The Seabury Press, 1957.

Spicer, Dorothy Gladys, *Children's Prayers from Other Lands.* New York: Association Press, 1955.

"St. Francis' Prayer," in *Masterpieces of Religious Verse,* edited by James D. Morrison. New York: Harper & Brothers, 1948.

Taylor, Florence, *Thine Is the Glory.* Philadelphia: The Westminster Press, 1962. Clarifies the meaning of the Lord's Prayer. (Primary.)

Wolcott, Carolyn M., *I Can Talk with God.* New York: Abingdon Press, 1962.

Saints

Farjeon, Eleanor, *Ten Saints.* New York: Henry Z. Walck, 1936. Includes, among others, St. Francis, St. Christopher, St. Nicholas, and St. Bridget.

Godden, Rumer, *St. Jerome and the Lion.* New York: The Viking Press, 1961. The story of the translator of the Bible into "people's Latin" and of his friendship with a lion. Told with gay, poetic beauty.

Jewett, Sophie, *God's Troubadour*. New York: Thomas Y. Crowell, 1938. Illustrations, in black and white, from Giotto's frescoes in Assisi, which inspired the book.

Politi, Leo, *St. Francis and the Animals*. New York: Charles Scribner's Sons, 1959. Charming illustrations in color by the author.

Stories and Storytelling

Brown, Jeannette Perkins, *The Storyteller in Religious Education*. Boston: The Pilgrim Press, 1951. Contains both a bibliography and a number of stories printed in full, including *The Legend of the Black Madonna*, by Margaret Applegarth.

Jacobs, Leland B., *Using Literature with Young Children*. New York: Teachers College Press (Columbia University), 1965.

Tooze, Ruth, *Storytelling*. Englewood Cliffs, N.J.: Prentice-Hall, 1959. Contains an excellent bibliography for a wide variety of stories.

Stories of Attitude

Andersen, Hans Christian, *The Emperor's New Clothes*. New York: Harcourt, Brace & World, 1959. Translated from the Danish and illustrated by Erik Blevgad. Delightful in every respect. (6-10 Years.)

—— *The Swineherd*. New York: Harcourt, Brace & World, 1958. "Notable children's book for 1958." The girl who cared more for material things than natural beauty lost the prince.

Anderson, Commander William R., *First Under the North Pole*. Cleveland: World Publishing Company, 1959. The voyage of the Nautilus. (Junior.)

Anglund, Joan Walsh, *Love Is a Special Way of Feeling*. New York: Harcourt, Brace & World, 1963. (All Ages.)

Bergaust, Erik, *First Men in Space*. New York: G. P. Putnam's Sons, 1960.

Dalgliesh, Alice, *Ride on the Wind*. New York: Charles Scribner's Sons, 1956. A retelling for children of *The Spirit of St. Louis*.

DeJong, Meindert, *Along Came a Dog*. New York: Harper & Brothers, 1958. A dog's desire to serve wins the approval of the other animals in his new home before it convinces the farmer.

———— *The Wheel on the School*. New York: Harper & Brothers, 1954. The Newberry Award book for that year. The children in a schoolroom have a dream of attracting storks to the roof of their schoolhouse, and are encouraged by their teacher: ". . . first to dream and then to do, isn't that the way to make a dream come true?"

Farjeon, Eleanor, *Mrs. Malone*. New York: Henry Z. Walck, 1962.

Fisher, Aileen, *Where Does Everyone Go?* New York: Thomas Y. Crowell, 1961. Charming poetry and illustrations about the fall and winter and a little boy's wondering.

Kennedy, John F., *Profiles in Courage*. New York: Harper & Row, 1961. Abridged for youth. (Older Junior.)

Krauss, Ruth, *Charlotte and the White Horse*. New York: Harper & Brothers, 1955. Illustrations by Maurice Sendak.

McNeer, May, and Ward, Lynd K., *Armed with Courage*. New York: Abingdon Press, 1957.

Seuss, Dr., *Horton Hears a Who!* New York: Random House, 1954. A Junior Literary Guild selection. The elephant goes to great trouble to protect some small creatures who live on a speck of dust. "A person is a person no matter how small."

Stillman, Peter, *That Happy Feeling of Thank You*. Norwalk, Conn.: The C. R. Gibson Company, 1964.

To Stimulate Awareness

Carson, Rachel, *The Sense of Wonder*. New York: Harper & Row, 1965. To help keep alive a child's ability to wonder. Beautifully illustrated with photographs.

Grifalconi, Ann, *City Rhythms*. New York: The Bobbs-Merrill Company, 1965. (Primary.)

Wolff, Janet, "The Imagination Books" (a series for ages 4-7). New York: E. P. Dutton & Company: *Let's Imagine Being*

Places, 1961; *Let's Imagine Sounds,* 1962; *Let's Imagine Colors,* 1963; *Let's Imagine Thinking Up Words,* 1965.

To Increase Understanding

Aliki, *A Weed Is a Flower.* Englewood Cliffs, N.J.: Prentice-Hall, 1965. The life of George Washington Carver. (Primary.)

Carlson, Natalie Savage, *The Empty Schoolhouse.* New York: Harper & Row, 1965. A realistic portrayal of problems of school integration in a small Louisiana town.

Caudil, Rebecca, *A Certain Small Shepherd.* New York: Holt, Rinehart & Winston, 1965. The story of a mute child's Christmas in Appalachia.

Clayton, Ed, *Martin Luther King, the Peaceful Warrior.* Englewood Cliffs, N.J.: Prentice-Hall, 1965. Enlarged edition with chapter on the 1964 Nobel Peace Prize. (Junior.)

DeJong, Meindert, *House of Sixty Fathers.* New York: Harper & Brothers, 1956. The effect of World War II in China on a child deserted and alone. (Older Junior.)

Garfield, James B., *Follow My Leader.* New York: The Viking Press, 1957. The story of a boy blinded by an accident. How he overcomes his handicap, with the help of a guide dog, to live with courage a busy, happy life. Has honesty and humor. (Junior.)

Krauss, Ruth, *I'll Be You and You Be Me.* New York: Harper & Brothers, 1956. Rhymes and sayings about friends, life, love, in the style of small children.

Pintoff, Ernest, *Always Help a Bird* (especially with a broken leg). New York: Harper & Row, 1965.

Saint-Exupéry, Antoine de, *The Little Prince.* New York: Reynal & Hitchcock, 1943. Translated from the French by Katherine Woods. A whimsical and grave story, not to be forgotten. (Junior and Adult.)

Travers, P. L., *The Fox at the Manger.* New York: W. W. Norton & Company, 1962. An unusual Christmas story by the author of *Mary Poppins.*

Films

Children Without. 16mm, 29 minutes, black and white. Produced by the National Education Association. Shows home and school life of deprived children, and although any film would be too short to treat the subject adequately, this one does give some basis for understanding and indicates to a degree the direction that teaching deprived children must take. May be borrowed from state education associations for a low fee or possibly for return postage. Those wishing to purchase it, may do so for $35.00 through the National Education Association, 1201 Sixteenth Street N.W., Washington, D.C. 20036. (Adult.)

Children Who Draw. 16mm, 44 minutes, black and white, combined with color. Rental: $15.00. An excellent documentary of children painting and drawing, produced in Japan. Distributor: Brandon Films, Inc., 200 West 57th Street, New York, N.Y. 10019.

The Coming of Christ. 16mm, 30 minutes, color. Rental: $15.00. A magnificent presentation using great art with authentic narration. Agency: Encyclopaedia Britannica Films, Inc., 38 West 32nd Street, New York, N.Y. 10001.

My Own Backyard to Play In. 16mm, 7 minutes, black and white. Rental: $15.00. An effective document of children playing among tenements and cluttered vacant lots in New York City. A plea for adequate play space, and an aid to understanding. (Adult.) Distributor: Edward Harrison, 1501 Broadway, New York, N.Y. 10036.

The Purple Turtle. 16mm, 13 minutes, color, sound. Available without charge. A lively short film of children drawing and painting. Although they are of preschool age, the principle of involvement illustrated applies to primary children. (Adult.) Address: The American Crayon Company, 167 Wayne Street, Jersey City, N.J. 07302.

The Puppet Films. 16mm, 15 minutes, black and white, or

color. Rental: $5.00 and $7.50. Produced by the National Council of Churches, Broadcasting and Film Commission, 1950-52. Available from denominational and other BFC film libraries. This is a series of nine films altogether. Especially recommended are those about the parables: *The Good Samaritan, The Lost Sheep* (including *The Lost Coin*), *The Prodigal Son,* and *The Ten Talents.* They delight children with their charm and dignity. A word of caution: they were produced several years ago and should be checked in advance for scratches and the like.

God's Wonder Series. 16mm, 10 minutes each, color. Produced by Church Craft Pictures, 3312 Lindell Boulevard, St. Louis, Mo., 63103. Rental: $5.00 each, from Religious Film Libraries; in New York: 17 Park Place, 10007. Titles in the series of eight: *God's Wonders on the Farm; God's Wonders in the Zoo; God's Wonders in Your Own Back Yard; God's Wonders in Flowers; God's Wonders in the Forest; God's Wonders in a Woodland Brook; God's Wonders in a Country Pond; God's Wonders in the Meadow.*

The photography is excellent, providing close-up views well worth seeing a second time. Could be used in relation to simple worship and as motivation for painting. Unfortunately, many questions are answered in advance, so that children's own exploration is somewhat curtailed. (Primary or Young Junior Groups.)

Helen Keller in Her Story. 16mm, 45 minutes, black and white. Rental: $12.50. Available without charge from some public libraries. A rare and moving documentary, it includes memorable scenes with Katharine Cornell, Martha Graham, Dwight D. Eisenhower, and others, as Miss Keller's own life of courage, faith, and perseverance is portrayed. An Academy Award winner. Distributor: Contemporary Films, 267 West 25th Street, New York, N.Y. 10001.

Mrs. Robin's Family. 16mm, 10 minutes, black and white, sound. Rental: $2.50 for three days. Produced by Coronet Instructional Films, 65 E. South Water Street, Chicago, Ill. 60601.

Check local outlets. The story of a robin family from early spring to late fall. Shows members of the family depending on each other. Good close-ups.

Bushy the Squirrel. General information the same as above. Excitement and fun as a boy makes friends with a squirrel. Other woodland animals also pictured.

Films to Stimulate Imagination

Begone Dull Care. 16mm, 9 minutes, color. Rental: $6.00. A visual poem of colorful abstractions by Norman McLaren. Music played by the Oscar Peterson Trio is an integral part of the film. (All Ages.)

Lines Horizontal. 16mm, 6 minutes, color. Rental: $6.00. An experiment in pure design. Lines move on screen in response to music played by Pete Seeger. (All Ages.) To borrow either of the two films above, address: Contemporary Films, Inc., 267 West 25th Street, New York, N.Y. 10001; or 614 Davis Street, Evanston, Ill. 60201; or 1211 Polk Street, San Francisco, Calif. 94109. Also, William M. Dennis Film Libraries, 2506½ West 7th Street, Los Angeles, Calif. 90057.

Lines Vertical. 16mm, 6 minutes, color. Rental: $6.00. Lines ruled directly on the film move with precision and grace against a background of changing colors in response to electronic piano music. Information on borrowing this film may be obtained from the International Film Bureau, 332 South Michigan Avenue, Chicago, Ill. 60604.

Note: Before ordering a film, it will be wise to check first with local rental agencies. Public libraries may have a free copy.

For further materials: *The Audio-Visual Resource Guide for Use in Religious Education,* published by the National Council of Churches, 475 Riverside Drive, New York, N.Y. 10027, is available at most denominational bookstores.

Recordings

Early Church Music
Gregorian Chant: *Missa De Angelis* and *Missa Cum Jubilo* (Gregorian Institute of America, PX-2)
Music of the Middle Ages (Haydn Society Records, HSE-9100)
Palestrina: *Missa Papae Marcelli* (Archive, 3074)

18th and 19th Centuries
Bach: *The Eight Little Preludes and Fugues* (Columbia, ML-5078). E. Power Biggs, playing classical organs of Europe.
Bach, Haydn, and others: *An 18th Century Concert* (Vanguard, BG-589). Includes Corelli's *Christmas Concerto,* Haydn's *Toy Symphony,* and Bach's *Jesu, Joy of Man's Desiring.*
Beethoven: *Symphony No. 9 in D Minor.* The last movement contains the "Ode to Joy" on which is based the hymn "Joyful, Joyful, We Adore Thee."
Saint-Saëns: *Carnival of the Animals*
Tchaikovsky: *Nutcracker Suite; Swan Lake* ("The Dance of the Little Swans" is recommended for its simplicity.)
Vivaldi: *The Four Seasons*

Contemporary
Grofé, Ferde: *Grand Canyon Suite.* The section "Sunrise" suggests new beginnings; "On the Trail," a journey; "Cloudburst," excitement.
Taylor, Deems: *Through the Looking Glass* (Olympian, MG-50081). The Eastman-Rochester Symphony Orchestra playing music based on Lewis Carroll's story. Recommended for humor: the section "Looking Glass Insects," in which the bee turns out to be an elephant!

Christmas Records
Carols Sung by the Bach Choir
Christmas Hymns and Carols, sung by the Robert Shaw Chorale
Christmas Songs, sung by the Obernkirche Children's Choir (Angel, 65021)

Menotti, Gian-Carlo: *Amahl and the Night Visitors.* Especially: Amahl playing his shepherd's pipe. The King's Song: How Far, How Far, My Crystal Star? The Shepherd's Dance.

Miscellaneous

Music for Children, by Carl Orff and Gunild Keetman (Angel, 35651). Experimentation with rhythms, musical instruments, the sound of both music and words.

Salli Terri: *Songs of Enchantment* (Capitol, 8482). Includes Brahms' "Lullaby," Humperdinck's "Prayer" from *Hänsel and Gretel,* "Mister Froggie Went a Courtin'," etc.

Sounds of the Sea (Folkways, 6121)

Sounds of a Tropical Rain Forest in America (Folkways, 6120). Produced for the American Museum of Natural History.

Slides

Slide collections can be borrowed without charge from the National Gallery, including a set of forty on the Christmas story in art, and one of fifty on Easter. Many museums have slides for sale, as do cathedrals both here and abroad. For example, from Coventry, England, one can order a view of the great west window of clear etched glass or the modern window behind the baptismal font from Bethlehem. A hand-picked collection in a church school can add to appreciation of both art and worship.

For other information, write to:

Christian Art
Visual Education Service
The Divinity School, Yale University
Box L 409, New Haven, Conn.

Extension Service
National Gallery of Art
Washington, D.C. 20565

Television

Our Inheritance in the Church, produced under the auspices of the Children's Work Committee of the Greater Portland Council of Churches in cooperation with KGW-TV, for a period of 13 weeks. A mimeographed copy of the plan may be procured for 25 cents by writing to the Greater Portland Council of Churches, 0245 Southwest Bancroft Street, Portland, Oregon 97201.

Traveling Exhibits

Reproductions of great art are on loan from the National Gallery of Art. Address: Extension Service, National Gallery of Art, Washington, D.C. 20565.

APPENDIX

Biblical Stories Related to Themes and Hymns

The material below is not intended to be presented to children as abstract themes or subthemes, but as thrilling events in the life of the world and of people as God moves to confirm through them his love and glory.

CREATION

In the Beginning:

Genesis 1:1-31; 2:1-3

HYMNS:

"Let the Whole Creation Cry"
by Stopford Brooke, 1832-1916
TUNE: Salzburg

"This Is My Father's World"
by Maltbie Babcock, 1858-1901
TUNE: Terra Beata

The Birth of Jesus:

Luke 1:26-35; 2:1-20; Matthew 2:1-12

HYMNS:

"O Come, O Come, Emmanuel"
Latin, c. 9th century
TUNE: Veni Emmanuel

"As with Gladness Men of Old"
by William C. Dix, 1837-1898
TUNE: Dix

"O Little Town of Bethlehem"
by Phillips Brooks, 1835-1893
TUNE: St. Louis

"Silent Night"
by Joseph Mohr, 1792-1848
TUNE: Stille Nacht (Franz Gruber)

"Hark! The Herald Angels Sing"
by Charles Wesley, 1707-1788
TUNE: Mendelssohn

The Birth of the Church:

Acts 1:12-14; 2:1-8, 12-14, 22-24, 33, 36-39, 41-42, 46-47

HYMNS:
> "God of Grace and God of Glory"
> > by Harry Emerson Fosdick, 1878
> > TUNE: Cwm Rhondda
>
> "Lord, I Want to Be a Christian"
> > Negro Spiritual
>
> "The Church's One Foundation"
> > by Samuel J. Stone, 1839-1900
> > TUNE: Aurelia

RECONCILIATION (RESCUE, RESTORATION)

Devotion:

The Psalms, chosen for strong feeling or imagery: 23; 24:1-10; 46:1-3, 10, 11; 51:10-12; 67; 100; 103:1-5, 10-12; 104: 1-4, 10-14, 19-25, 27, 35; 121; 139: 1-4, 23-24; 148

The "Doxology" of the Psalter: Psalm 150

The Lord's Prayer: Matthew 6:9-13; Luke 11:1-4

Rescue:

The Parable of the Good Samaritan: Luke 10:25-37

The Parables of the Lost Sheep and the Lost Coin: Luke 15:1-10

HYMNS:
> "The Lord's My Shepherd"
> > Based on Psalm 23 (Scottish Psalter, 1650)
> > TUNE: Crimond
>
> "Saviour, Like a Shepherd Lead Us"
> > Anon. 1794
> > TUNE: Sicilian Mariners

Faith:

The Story of Abraham: Genesis, Chapters 13, 15, 17, 18, 21

The Story of Noah: Genesis, Chapters 6 through 9:17

David and Goliath: I Samuel, Chapter 17

Moses: From Exodus, Chapters 1 through 13; 15; 16; 18 through 20; 24 through 27; 29; 35; 36; 39; 40

The Fiery Furnace: From Daniel 3:1-28

Bartimaeus, the Blind Man: Mark 10:46-52

The Centurion and the Slave: Luke 7:1-10

HYMNS:

"The God of Abraham Praise"
Revised version of the "Yigdal,"
a Jewish Doxology
TUNE: Leoni (Traditional Hebrew)
"When Israel Was in Egypt's Land"
Negro Spiritual
TUNE: Go Down Moses (Negro melody)

Fellowship:

"Let the Children Come": Mark 10:13-16
Jesus Washes the Disciples' Feet: John 13:1-17
The Last Supper: Matthew 26:17-28
The Risen Christ: From Luke 24; John 21; Matthew 28

HYMNS:

"I Love to Think that Jesus Saw"
by Ada Skemp, 1857-1927
TUNE: Childhood
"In Christ There Is No East or West"
by John Oxenham, 1852-1941
TUNE: St. Peter
"Let All Mortal Flesh Keep Silence"
From the Liturgy of St. James
TUNE: Picardy

Judgment:

Adam and Eve Driven from the Garden: Genesis 3
Amos Warns Israel: From Amos, Chapters 1, 5, 7
Jerusalem Destroyed: From II Kings, Chapters 24, 25; Jeremiah 40
Cleansing the Temple: Mark 11:15-18
The Crucifixion: Matthew 27; Mark 15:39; Luke 23:33-49; John 19:25-30

Forgiveness:

Joseph and His Brothers: From Genesis, Chapters 37; 39: 1-12, 16-21; 40 through 46:7
Jonah: The Book of Jonah
The Parable of the Prodigal Son: Luke 15:11-32

The Parable of the Pharisee and the Tax Gatherer: Luke
18:9-14

The Story of Zacchaeus: Luke 19:1-10

The Crucifixion: From Matthew 27; Mark 15:39; Luke
23:33-49; John 19:25-30

HYMNS:

"Were You There?"
Negro Spiritual
TUNE: Were You There

"There's a Wideness in God's Mercy"
by Frederick Faber, 1814-1863
TUNE: In Babilone

Commitment:

David Serves Saul: From I Samuel, Chapters 16, 18, 20, 26,
31

David as King: From II Samuel, Chapters 2, 5, 7, 8; I Kings,
Chapter 2

Isaiah's Call in the Temple: Isaiah 6:1-8

Jeremiah's Call to Prophecy: Jeremiah 1:1-9; 7:2-11

Jeremiah Is Accused of Treason: Jeremiah, Chapters 37, 38

Jesus' Baptism and Temptation: Matthew 3 through 4:11

Jesus Calls the Disciples: Mark 1; Matthew 4

The Entry into Jerusalem: Mark 11:1-10

The Garden of Gethsemane: Matthew 26:36-46

Peter Confesses Christ: Luke 9:18-20

The "Great Commission": Matthew 28:16-20

HYMNS:

"Once to Every Man and Nation"
by James Russell Lowell, 1819-1891
TUNE: Ebenezer (Ton-y-Botel)

"I Sing a Song of the Saints of God"
by Lesbia Scott, 1898-
TUNE: Grand Isle

"He Who Would Valiant Be"
by John Bunyan, 1628-1688
TUNE: St. Dunstan's

FULFILLMENT

The Israelites Enter the Promised Land: Joshua 1:1-6; 21; 24

Jerusalem Is Rebuilt: Nehemiah 1, 2, 4, 6

Parable of the Five Talents: Matthew 25:14-30

Parable of the Mustard Seed: Matthew 13:31-32

The Resurrection: Mark 16:1-8

Peter Becomes a "Rock" of Faith: John 21:15-18; Acts, Chapters 1 through 5; 10; 11

The Promise: "Behold I make all things new": Revelation 21:1-5a, 22-26; 22:1-5

The Early Church: The Acts of the Apostles

Painting Projects

A Primary Group (One Hour)

The class has been thinking together about prayer, with special emphasis on the meaning of the Lord's Prayer. They have had conversations and activities related to the Bible and three other books: "I Can Talk with God," "Tell Me About Prayer," and "Thine Is the Glory." They have heard the Bible account of Jesus teaching the disciples how to pray, and have sung the song "Jesus Was a Loving Teacher," No. 85 in *Hymns for Primary Worship*. They have also heard the Friendship Press stories "The Swimming Pool" and "The Apple Tree House" which deal with the meaning of "Our" Father, and they have tried creative rhythm based on the Lord's Prayer. A small group of children has been doing special work on this with one of the teachers, and plans to present it on the last day of the unit during worship. They will use the musical setting by Malotte. If Helen Brown does not have to sing in Youth Choir that morning, she will come and sing it for the children. Another group is planning a litany. All have been told that on this final day the schedule will be different. Worship will come first, and immediately afterward, at tables already prepared, they will have an opportunity to paint their thoughts and feelings about the Lord's Prayer.

A Junior Group (Extended Session)

These children have had several sessions on faith in relation to the life of the Church. They have learned of people in the Old and New Testaments, as well as later, who have shown the qualities that are essential for the work of the Church. The teacher is giving an entire morning to painting as a recapitulation of the meaning of faith. To save time for the actual activity, the group (which is an enthusiastic one of fourth-graders) planned a week ahead of time what they wanted to do. They chose the five persons who, in their opinion, represent the "best" in faith that they have heard about so far: Abraham, Jesus, St. Paul, St. Francis, and Martin Luther. Further, they decided, with a few suggestions from their teacher, that they wanted to do the paintings in the shape of Gothic windows on large brown mural paper because they wanted to paint big. Each child chose which one of the five he wants to work on, and a leader was appointed for each group.

Everyone who could, came unusually early on the Sunday when the painting was scheduled, and interest ran high all morning. At the end there were "windows" on faith, not transparent to be sure, but giving a great deal of satisfaction to the children when they put them up around their walls. Abraham was kneeling in prayer at an altar of stones, Jesus was preaching from a boat, Paul was "seeing the light" in a strong ray from the sky, St. Francis was talking with the birds and a wolf, Luther was "taking his stand."

Had this project been done in a one-hour session, it would have been unfinished, but could have been completed the following week.

Brief Suggestions for Class Projects

1. Abstract designs based on:
   The Parables
      The Lost Coin
      The Lost Sheep
      The Good Samaritan
      The Prodigal Son
      The Mustard Seed

The Psalms

The message of one or several of the prophets: the fiery furnace for Daniel, the plumb line for Amos, the ravens for Elijah, the whale for Jonah, etc.

2. Background settings for creative dramatizations of stories

3. Celebration of Christmas or Easter through art

4. Completion of an open-end story

5. Creation:

   Each "day" can be given a separate session. On the day of the "waters," listen to the Folkways recording *Sounds of the Sea*. On the day of the "living creatures" or "vegetation," the Folkways recording *Sounds of a South American Rain Forest* can be stimulating.

6. Compose an original litany and paint the meaning of the response or one of the statements of praise or petition.

7. The Lord's Prayer:

   Be sure the class knows its meaning. Group the phrases with them. Try interpreting them in rhythmic movement (their own spontaneous suggestions). Let each child choose a phrase to paint.

8. Mural based on church architecture through the ages:
   A house in Palestine
   The catacombs
   A cathedral
   A meeting house
   A modern building

9. Mural based on the lives of saints or missionaries

10. Mural based on a variety of contributions to church history: apostles, artists, architects (cathedrals), inventor (Gutenberg, the printing press), reformers (Luther, Calvin, Wesley), monks, scholars, writers, etc.

11. Our own church:
   Visit the church. Go in silence and sit together without talking, thinking of what the church means to the children. Then let them share some of their thoughts before returning to the classroom to paint about the "trip." At another session, go outside together; look at the church building, walking around it if possible. Think of what it means or can mean to the neighborhood. Return and paint.

12. Scenes from the life of Luther:
   The storm that changed his life
   Reading the chained Bible in the monastery
   Nailing the theses to the church door
   The kidnaping
   "Here I Stand"

13. "Windows" based on any Biblical theme such as faith: A class series could include Abraham, Daniel, Moses, Jesus, St. Paul, St. Francis, etc. The class will enjoy discussion to choose their own series.

14. Service projects:
   Take a "gallery" of paintings to a children's ward at a hospital or a home for elderly people.
   Plan an offering for the blind after reading stories of Helen Keller and seeing the documentary film on her life. Paint in response. After such an experience, one boy said he wanted to "paint a landscape to the glory of God." And he did.

15. Take a "beauty walk" and paint in response.

16. Other non-Biblical motivation:
   Paintings based on experiences of beauty, compassion, joy, laughter, sadness, thanksgiving, wonder, etc.
   Paintings inspired by daily living, music, poetry, rhythm, or trouble

Pictures

The Advent Season

"The Annunciation," Fra Filippo Lippi (Metropolitan)

"Adoration of the Shepherds," Giorgione (National Gallery)

"Adoration of the Magi," Botticelli (National Gallery)

"The Eve of St. Nicholas," Jan Steen (Rijksmuseum, Amsterdam)

"The Journey of the Magi," Sassetta (Metropolitan)

"Joseph and the Christ Child," Tiepolo (Detroit)

"Nativity," De La Tour (Louvre)

"The Flight into Egypt," Tiepolo (San Diego)

"Rest on the Flight into Egypt," David (National Gallery)

"Presentation of the Christ Child in the Temple," Jan Proost (Denver)

The Ministry of Christ

"The Life of Christ," a charming booklet illustrated by prints of the great paintings at the Detroit Institute of Arts

"Christ Healing the Sick," Johannes Jurres (St. Louis)

"Christ with the Sick Around Him, Receiving Little Children," an etching by Rembrandt, one of a set of four (Metropolitan)

"Christ at the Sea of Galilee," Tintoretto (National Gallery)

"Christ Healing the Blind," School of Van Dyck (Sacramento)

"Jesus Among the Children," Emil Nolde (Museum of Modern Art)

"The Temptation of Christ," Duccio (Frick Collection)

"The Purification of the Temple," El Greco (Frick Collection)

"Christ and the Fishermen," Rouault (Reproductions, New York Graphic Society)

"The Last Supper," André Derain (Chicago)

"The Last Supper," Andrea del Sarto (Florence)

"Agony in the Garden," early School of Florence (Detroit)

"The Crucifixion," George Bellows (Cleveland)

"Christ at Emmaus," Rembrandt (Copenhagen)

"The Friend of the Humble" (Supper at Emmaus), Lhermitte (Boston)

Parables
"The Good Samaritan," Fetti (Metropolitan)
"The Good Samaritan," Van Gogh (National Gallery)
"The Prodigal Son," William Morris Hunt (Boston)
"Return of the Prodigal Son," Murillo (National Gallery)
"Return of the Prodigal Son," J. L. Forain (National Gallery)
"Return of the Prodigal," Rembrandt (Hermitage, Leningrad)

Apostles
"The Calling of the Apostles Peter and Andrew," Duccio (National Gallery)
"The Apostle Paul," Rembrandt (National Gallery)

Saints
"St. Francis Conferring His Cloak," Giotto (Assisi, Italy)
"St. George and the Dragon," Raphael (National Gallery)
"St. Martin and the Beggar," El Greco (National Gallery)

Animals
"Cow Grazing," John B. Allston (Boston)
"The Newborn Calf," John B. Allston (Boston)
"The Crowing Cock," Rubens and J. Wildens (Aachen)
"The Enemy" (A falcon swooping down to catch a duckling), Hondecoeter (Metropolitan)
"Sheep Returning from Pasture," Constable (Boston)
"Sleeping Gypsy" (with lion), Rousseau (Museum of Modern Art)
"Study of a Young Hare," Albrecht Dürer (Albertina, Vienna)
"A Little Owl," Albrecht Dürer (Reproductions, Metropolitan)
"Three Puppies," Gauguin (Museum of Modern Art)

People
"The Angelus," Jean François Millet (Louvre)
"Le Bénédicité" (The Blessing), Chardin (Louvre)
"Boy with a Book," James Chapin (Reproductions, New York Graphic Society)

"Boys in a Pasture," Winslow Homer (Boston)
"Girl at the Open Half-Door," Rembrandt (Chicago)
"A Girl with a Watering Can," Renoir (National Gallery)
"The Gleaners," Jean François Millet (Louvre)
"The Gourmet," Picasso (National Gallery)
"Gypsy Woman with Baby," Modigliani (National Gallery)
"Mother and Child," Picasso (Baltimore)
"Motherhood," James Chapin (Reproductions, New York Graphic Society)
"People and Dog in Sun," Joan Miró (Basel, Switzerland)
"The Prayer," Nicholas Maes (Rijksmuseum, Amsterdam)
"Third Class Carriage," Daumier (Metropolitan)
"Street Scene," Vermeer (Rijksmuseum, Amsterdam)
"The Tragedy," Picasso (National Gallery)
"The Washerwomen," Renoir (Baltimore)
"Young Girl Peeling Apples," Nicholas Maes (Metropolitan)
"We Greet Thee, Mary," Gauguin (Metropolitan)

Miscellaneous
"The Birthday," Marc Chagall (Guggenheim)
"Breezing Up," Winslow Homer (National Gallery)
"Christian Nocturne," Rouault (Louvre)
"Country School," Winslow Homer (St. Louis)
"The Green Violinist," Marc Chagall (Guggenheim)
"Indian Story," Paul Klee (Reproductions, Shorewood Publishers)
"The Kitchen," Edouard Vuillard (Metropolitan)
"Northeaster," Winslow Homer (Metropolitan)
"Old Settlers, Adirondacks," Winslow Homer (Boston)
"Rising Storm," George Inness (Boston)
"A Sunday Afternoon on the Grande Jatte," Georges Seurat (Chicago)
"Sunflowers," Monet (Metropolitan)
"Sunflowers," Van Gogh (Tate, London)
"The Starry Sky," Van Gogh (Museum of Modern Art)

Note: Prints and reproductions of the originals are often available at art shops as well as at the museums. For a list of 95 museums in the United States and Canada, with some of the reproductions available at each, see *Art Reproductions,* compiled by Jane Clapp. New York: Scarecrow Press, 1961.

Museums in the United States

Arkansas Museum of Fine Arts, Little Rock, Arkansas.

The Art Institute of Chicago, Michigan Avenue at Adams Street, Chicago, Illinois.

Seattle Art Museum, Volunteer Park, Seattle, Washington.

Museum of Fine Arts, 469 Huntington Avenue, Boston, Massachusetts.

California Palace of the Legion of Honor, Lincoln Park, San Francisco, California.

Cincinnati Art Museum, Eden Park, Cincinnati, Ohio.

City Museum of Art, Forest Park, St. Louis, Missouri.

Cleveland Museum of Art, 11150 East Boulevard, Cleveland, Ohio.

The Cloisters, Fort Tryon Park, New York, New York.

E. B. Crocker Art Gallery, 216 O Street, Sacramento, California.

Denver Art Museum, 1343 Acoma, Denver, Colorado.

The Detroit Institute of Arts, 5200 Woodward Avenue, Detroit, Michigan.

M. H. De Young Memorial Museum, Golden Gate Park, San Francisco, California.

Evansville Museum of Arts and Sciences, 411 Southeast River Drive, Evansville, Indiana.

The Fine Arts Gallery of San Diego, Balboa Park, San Diego, California.

The Frick Collection, 1 East 70th Street, New York, New York.

The Solomon R. Guggenheim Museum, Fifth Avenue at 89th Street, New York, New York.

The Hyde Collection, 161 Warren Street, Glens Falls, New York.

Los Angeles County Museum, Exposition Park, Los Angeles, California.

The Metropolitan Museum of Art, Fifth Avenue at 82nd Street, New York, New York.

Museum of Modern Art, 11 West 53rd Street, New York, New York.

National Gallery of Art, Sixth Street and Constitution Avenue, Washington, D.C.

Norfolk Museum, Museum Plaza, Norfolk, Virginia.

North Carolina Museum of Art, 107 East Morgan Street, Raleigh, North Carolina.

Philadelphia Museum of Art, 719 Catharine Street, Philadelphia, Pennsylvania.

Walker Art Center, 1710 Lyndale Avenue South, Minneapolis, Minnesota.

Worcester Art Museum, 55 Salisbury Street, Worcester, Massachusetts.

This list is only partial. There are, of course, many others that travelers will enjoy visiting and that families can plan to include. See *Museums Directory of the United States and Canada,* edited by Erwin O. Christensen. Washington, D.C.: American Association of Museums, 1961. Gives information on collections as well as hours and admission fees, where applicable.

Where to Order Reproductions

Art Museums: Museums often sell reproductions of their own originals in post-card size for 10 cents, or 25 cents for a larger size. Still larger sizes, suitable for framing, are sometimes available. Write for listings, specifying that you would like a separate listing of religious subjects if one is available.

Art Reproductions, 50 West 42nd Street, New York, New York 10036.

Artext Prints, Inc., Westport, Connecticut.

Prints of varied sizes from "Juniors" at 3 cents each to those large enough for framing. Bulletins on request.

Boston Public Library, Copley Square, Boston, Massachusetts 02116. "Association Prints" of the John Singer Sargent "Frieze of the Prophets" available.

International Art Publishing Company, Inc., 243 West Congress Street, Detroit, Michigan 48226. Their collection of Alinari color prints includes "The Holy Night," by Marata, "Angels Dancing," by Fra Angelico, and many others, priced from $3.00.

Oestreichers, 43 West 46th Street, New York, New York 10036.

Penn Prints, 221 Park Avenue South, New York, New York 10003. Color prints by traditional and modern artists at $1.00 each; minimum order, $3.00.

Shorewood Publishers, 724 Fifth Avenue, New York, New York 10019. Illustrated catalogue, $1.00. Minimum order, $20.00.

The United Church of Christ Bookstore, 1505 Race Street, Philadelphia 5, Pennsylvania. Portfolios of pictures for primary and junior-age children.

New York Graphic Society, 95 Putnam Avenue, Greenwich, Connecticut 06831. Large illustrated catalogue at $25.00. Small catalogue of religious subjects on request.

The SPCK Bookstore, 69 Great Peter Street, London S.W.1, England. The Society for Promotion of Christian Knowledge distributes reproductions of great Christian art.

Something Different

Contemporary Christian Art, Inc., 1060 Lexington Avenue, New York, New York 10021. A gallery of modern work.

The Gallery, 85 Christopher Street, New York, New York 10014. The artist Irwin Rosenhouse shows his own work. His portrayals of children lift the heart, and some reproductions are available in greeting-card form.

AUTHOR'S NOTES

Chapter 1: For Joy

1. Ruth Mock, *Principles of Art Teaching*, p. 7.
2. Slogan of the John C. Campbell Folk School, Brasstown, North Carolina.
3. A 15-minute film of preschool children drawing and painting. Available without charge from the American Crayon Company, 167 Wayne Street, Jersey City, New Jersey.
4. The original is at the Museum of Modern Art, 11 West 53rd Street, New York, New York 10019. Post-card prints in color are available for 10 cents each.

Chapter 2: For Acceptance

1. In *The Arts in the Classroom*, Natalie Robinson Cole gives interesting examples of her use of creative writing with deprived children.
2. *The Meaning of Persons*, p. 182.

Chapter 3: For Growth and Understanding

1. *Philosophy in a New Key*, p. 41.
2. Daniel Mendelowitz, *Children are Artists* (1953 Edition), p. 24.
3. *Principles of Art Teaching*, plate 11, facing p. 80.

Chapter 4: For Fellowship

1. Paul Tillich, "Creative Love in Education," in *World Christian Education*, Second Quarter, 1949 (reprinted 1964).
2. *Herein Is Love*, p. 29.
3. Hymn tune: "Lobe den Herren."
4. The children's Art Project of the Synod of Oregon of the United Presbyterian Church in the U.S.A. See Mary Elizabeth Thompson, "A Saturday Art Project," in *The Christian Educator*, Vol. 8, Jan./Mar., 1965.

Chapter 5: For Appreciation

1. *Your Child and His Art*, pp. 164-165.
2. *Ibid.*
3. New York: Thomas Nelson & Sons, 1963. Sponsored by the World Council of Christian Education and the Sunday School Association.

4. Imo Ruyle Foster, "Art Is Not a Luxury," in *The International Journal of Religious Education,* December, 1962, p. 16.

5. *Tunisian Watercolors and Drawings.* New York: Harry N. Abrams, 1959, p. 1.

6. *Surprised by Joy,* p. 7.

7. *Ibid.,* p. 6.

8. *Ibid.,* p. 10.

9. Pp. 171-172.

Chapter 6: In Any Kind of Parish

1. "What Migrant Farm Children Learn," in *Saturday Review,* May 15, 1965, p. 74.

2. *Education Through Art,* p. 70 (Revised Edition).

3. *Your Child and His Art,* p. 178.

Chapter 9: Subject Matter

1. "Creative Love in Education," in *World Christian Education,* Second Quarter, 1949 (reprinted 1964).

2. Seymour Siegel, "Martin Buber: A Seeker of World Brotherhood" in *United Synagogue Review,* October, 1965, p. 13.

3. For a step-by-step description of how one group prepared to dramatize the Joseph story, see Agnes Kemp, "The Joseph Story Through the Eyes of Eight-year-olds," in *The International Journal of Religious Education,* September, 1965.

4. See Samuel Terrien, *The Bible and the Church,* pp. 75-76.

GENERAL BIBLIOGRAPHY

On Art and Art Teaching

Adams, Henry, *Mont-Saint-Michel and Chartres.* New York: Houghton Mifflin Company, 1904.

Alschuler, Rose H., and Hattwick, La B. W., *Painting and Personality.* Chicago: University of Chicago Press, 1947.

"Art in Christian Education," Special Issue, *International Journal of Religious Education,* February, 1959.

Barr, Alfred H., Jr., *What Is Modern Painting?* New York: Museum of Modern Art, 1958.

Cole, Natalie Robinson, *The Arts in the Classroom.* New York: John Day Company, 1940.

Coles, Robert, "What Migrant Farm Children Learn," *Saturday Review,* May 15, 1965.

"Contemporary Art and Christian Education," Special Issue, *International Journal of Religious Education,* February, 1966.

D'Amico, Victor, and Wilson, Frances, *Art for the Family.* New York: Museum of Modern Art, distributed by Doubleday & Company, 1958.

Ellis, Richenda, *Natural Creativity in Children.* Menlo Park, Calif.: Institute for Editorial Research, 1964.

Gardner, Helen, *Art Through the Ages,* 4th edition. New York: Harcourt, Brace & Company, 1958.

Langer, Susanne K., *Philosophy in a New Key.* Cambridge, Mass.: Harvard University Press, 1942.

Leonard, Mary K., *Let's Create.* Athens, Ohio: Ohio University Elementary School, College of Education.

Linderman and Herberholz, *Developing Artistic and Perceptual Awareness.* Dubuque, Iowa: Wm. C. Brown Company, 1964.

Lowenfeld, Viktor, *Your Child and His Art.* New York: The Macmillan Company, 1954.

Tournier, Paul, *Creative and Mental Growth.* New York: The Macmillan Company, 1964 ed.

Mendelowitz, Daniel M., *Children Are Artists.* Stanford: Stanford University Press, 1953; 2nd edition, 1963.

Miller, Samuel H., "Works of Art Are Things in Themselves," *International Journal of Religious Education,* February, 1959, p. 16.

Mock, Ruth, *Principles of Art Teaching.* London: University of London Press, 1959.

Read, Herbert Edward, *Education Through Art.* New York: Pantheon Books, 1945; 3rd edition, revised, 1958.

Richardson, Marion, *Art and the Child.* London: University of London Press, 1948.

Scollon, Kenneth M., "Why Art in Education?" *Saturday Review*, February 15, 1964.
Thompson, Mary Elizabeth, "A Saturday Art Project," *The Christian Educator*, Vol. 8, Jan./Mar., 1965.
Young, Mary, *Singing Windows*. New York: Abingdon Press, 1962.

On Christian Life and Teaching

Ashton-Warner, Sylvia, *Teacher*. New York: Simon & Schuster, 1963.
Chaplin, Dora, *Children and Religion*. New York: Charles Scribner's Sons, 1948.
Howe, Reuel, *Herein Is Love*. Valley Forge, Pa.: Judson Press, 1961. (Paperback)
Lewis, C. S., *Surprised by Joy*. Harcourt, Brace & Company, 1955.
Stewart, James S., *The Life and Teachings of Jesus Christ*. New York: Harper & Brothers, 1958. (Cloth or Paperback) A British classic published in America.
Tennant, Roger, *Christ Encountered*. New York: The Seabury Press, 1966.
Tillich, Paul, "Creative Love in Education," in *World Christian Education*, Second Quarter, 1949. Reprinted 1964.
Tournier, Paul, *The Meaning of Persons*. New York: Harper & Brothers, 1957.

On Biblical Background

Goodspeed, Edgar J., *How Came the Bible*. New York: Abingdon Press, 1940.
James, Fleming, *Personalities of the Old Testament*. New York: Charles Scribner's Sons, 1939.
——— *Thirty Psalmists*. New York: The Seabury Press, 1965. (Paperback)
Muilenburg, James, *The Way of Israel*. New York: Harper & Brothers, 1961.
Swaim, J. Carter, *Where Our Bible Came From*. New York: Association Press, 1960. (A Reflection Book paperback, 50 cents.)
Terrien, Samuel, *The Bible and the Church*. Philadelphia: The Westminster Press, 1962.
Wedel, Theodore O., *The Drama of the Bible*. Cincinnati: Forward Movement Publications, 1965.
Wright, G. Ernest, *Shechem, the Biography of a Biblical City*. New York: The McGraw-Hill Book Company, 1965. For the person interested

in archaeology. Beginners will find Chapters 1 and 2 especially helpful in bringing alive the ancient site of Shechem.

Wright, G. Ernest, and Fuller, Reginald H., *The Book of the Acts of God.* New York: Doubleday & Company, 1957.

On the Church

Bowie, Walter Russell, *The Story of the Church.* New York: Abingdon Press, 1955.

Dawley, Powel Mills, *Chapters in Church History.* New York: The Seabury Press, 1950.

Wright, Robert Roy, *The Church's First Thousand Years.* New York: Abingdon Press, 1960.

On the Inner City

Loretan, Joseph O., and Umas, Shelley, *Teaching the Disadvantaged.* New York: Teacher's College Press (Columbia), 1966.

Riessman, Frank, *The Culturally Deprived Child.* New York: Harper & Row, 1962. A positive approach to the educational problems of these children, with some useful principles and methods.

On Research

Goldman, Ronald, *Religious Thinking from Childhood to Adolescence.* London: Routledge and Kegan Paul, 1964. A discussion of thirty years' findings in the field of children's religious concepts, by a member of the staff of King Alfred's College, Winchester, England, who is responsible for religious instruction.